SKETCH MAP
Shewing Indian Canoe route explored by
Mr G.M. DAWSON Geologist H.M.N.A.B.C

9-18-63

((43-12636)

LAC PLAT

WOODS

N.W. POINT

NORTHWEST ANGLE STA

White

CHILTENOUTH LAKE

Tumisrac Swamp

PORTAGE

CANOE ISLAND

OF THE

LAKE

BUFFALO PT

ST ROSEAU DEPOT

LAKE OF THE WOODS

LINE

Scale ‖ Miles

WEST ON THE 49th PARALLEL

WEST ON

NORTH
49°
LATITUDE

BRITISH AND UNITED STATES BOUNDARY COMMISSIONS 1872-4

THE 49th
PARALLEL

Red River to the Rockies
1872–1876

JOHN E. PARSONS

William Morrow and Company
New York 1963

For Dale and Ruth

TABLE OF CONTENTS

LIST OF ILLUSTRATIONS

FOREWORD

For nearly a century the boundary between the United States and Canada has been taken for granted, just as have peaceful relations between the two countries. While the slogan "54-40 or fight" is still remembered, its context in history or geography receives less understanding. This oversight or complacency is perhaps more marked in the States, but it exists in Canada too. A corollary assumption is that the border line between the two countries was as easy to locate as to define, with no serious problems of maintenance. Once more latitude has been made into platitude. So said a Chief Justice of Canada, while celebrating the centennial of naval disarmament on the Great Lakes: "In the new world the simplicity of a unit of latitude has sufficed. From the Lake of the Woods to the Pacific the 49th parallel is good enough for us. . . . Strategic frontiers are unnecessary where good faith and mutual trust prevail."

But the late Sir Charles Fitzpatrick, speaking on St. Patrick's Day in New York, had the tact not to mention the three times or more that Fenians from the United States crossed the line to invade Canada in years following the Civil War. They acted, of course, in emulation of the Confederates who in 1864 raided St. Albans, Vermont, from the Province of Quebec. The "undefended border" posed serious problems then, not only for those unexpectedly under attack but to the friendly country whence the raiders came. Just as these hostilities along the boundary have long since been forgotten, so have the initial difficulties of defining and tracing the line itself, if indeed they ever were fully appreciated.

Excepting Alaska, the last portion of the northern international boundary to be fixed on the ground was surveyed in 1872-76, from the Lake of the Woods to the Rocky Mountains. Of its location along the 49th parallel, an eminent geographer has written: "Seemingly the simplest of boundary types, geometrical lines actually may be difficult to define and often are difficult to demarcate." Just how hard the task was, and the problems and vicissitudes of the British, American and Canadian surveyors in relatively unexplored Indian country, provide the substance for this account. Among other things it explains why today only one boundary monument in a thousand stands precisely at 49 degrees north latitude.

The story has never before been told from diaries and letters written on the line, nor from more than one national viewpoint. Neither has the British Government's diplomatic effort to acquire the Northwest Angle at the Lake of the Woods been fully related, nor its earlier negotiation for Point Roberts at the western end of the parallel. Both met with American intransigence.

A further objective is to bring out the character of the participants in the survey as western pioneers in a real sense. The effective leaders on both sides were regular army engineers, their motives peaceful, professional and disinterested. With courage and co-operation they performed an arduous duty for the future tranquillity of their respective countries, traversing and mapping a frontier eight hundred miles long, most of it arid wilderness. Their work preceded the coming to the northwest of the Canadian Mounted Police and by several years the American campaign against the Sioux. In the writer's opinion, these engineers deserve to be remembered at least as well as more notorious men of violence in the west. Noteworthy, too, are the foibles of the actors in this first exercise in international harmony, after a long period of Anglo-American tension.

As will be seen the surveyors had little or nothing to do with the political decision as to where the international line should run. That question, except for afterthoughts about the Northwest Angle, had been determined by treaty more than fifty years previously. The boundary along the 49th parallel has been described as "antecedent" or "derived," that is to say, based on traditions or predilections held elsewhere than in the region bisected. At the time of division, the area contained hardly any civilized inhabitants, and precise knowledge of its natural features, such as waterways, elevations, game or travel routes, was scant. That the astronomical line selected has proved satisfactory in a functional sense is due less to any accidental resemblance to a "natural" boundary than to the good will toward each other of the people who came to settle the plains on either side.

No study of a topic as untouched as the history of the

49th parallel line, reaching into the archives of three countries, could have been developed without the help and favor of many persons. My interest was first aroused about ten years ago at the headquarters of the Royal Canadian Mounted Police, Ottawa, when Inspector Bayfield showed me some original photographs taken for the British Boundary Commission. I was writing a book on the Winchester rifle, and the pictures led to mention of its use by various participants in the 1872-76 survey. Their accounts, touching but incidentally on firearms, opened a far wider field for historical exploration.

One of these participants was Lieut. Francis Vinton Greene, U.S. Engineers, whose letters and sketchbook have most fortunately been preserved in the New York Public Library and the Yale University Library. To Mrs. Eleanor Greene Potter, his daughter, and her sisters Mrs. Gertrude Greene Bryant and Mrs. Edith Greene Lindley, as well as to the two libraries, I am most grateful for helpful interest and generous permission to quote. Both Robert W. Hill, Keeper of Manuscripts in the New York Public Library, and Archibald Hanna, Librarian of the Western Americana Collection at Yale, have been more than obliging.

For researches in England I am indebted to Adam Roberts, a student of history at Oxford with whom I was put in touch by my friend Sir Rodger Winn. Mr. Roberts diligently traced descendants of British participants in the survey, and it was entirely through his efforts that the letters of two Royal Engineers, Captain Anderson and Lieutenant Galwey, were found. The Anderson letters were sent on from New Zealand by Samuel Anderson Chaffey, a great-nephew, who merits many thanks for his willingness to place them permanently in the Yale Library. Mrs.

Rose Mary Galwey generously made available the letters of her late husband's father, and Mrs. Vera M. Wilson obligingly supplied documents concerning the career of her father, Lt. Col. Valentine F. Rowe, R.E. Like information as to Maj. Gen. Donald R. Cameron, R.A., was provided through the kindness of his daughter, Mrs. Sophie J. Gray.

In London Adam Roberts made many visits to the Public Record Office and the Foreign Office Library to locate and summarize official documents and reports. The Crown copyright maps used as end papers and the extracts from unpublished Crown copyright material in the Public Record Office have been reproduced by permission of the Controller, Her Majesty's Stationery Office.

In Washington, Edgar A. Klapp, Administrative Officer of the American Section, International Boundary Commission, United States and Canada, has been most obliging in providing information. Mr. Klapp very kindly put at my disposal a collection of early photographs, the original marker shown on the jacket, and a complete set of current boundary maps. At the National Archives I was given access in the Diplomatic Division to the official records of the American Boundary Commission of 1872-76 and to various military reports of that period in its Civil War Branch. At the Library of Congress I was able to examine the manuscript diary of Hamilton Fish when Secretary of State.

In Ottawa the Dominion Archivist W. Kaye Lamb and the Assistant Archivist Pierre Brunet afforded me much help in supplying copies of documents and photographs from the Public Archives of Canada and, through interlibrary loan, pertinent Foreign Office records on microfilm. These I was able to examine at the New-York Historical Society through the co-operation of its Director and Librarian, James J. Heslin, and the Chief of the Reading Room, Miss Geraldine Beard. It was indeed the remarkable memory of Wilmer R. Leech, the Society's Curator of Manuscripts, that led me to the collection of Greene letters at the New York Public Library.

Besides these many helpful sources, I have likewise to thank Miss Mary B. Millman, Associate Professor of Nursing at the University of Toronto, for permitting her father's album of survey photographs to be copied; S. James Gooding for locating significant correspondence in the Provincial Archives of Ontario; S. Basil Haw for research into British military records; the Gilcrease Institute of American History and Art at Tulsa, Oklahoma, for permission to reproduce sketches by William Cary; Miss Marie Baboyant of the Montreal City Library for access to the Gagnon Collection of Canadiana; Donald E. Thompson, Librarian of Wabash College, for data on the Twining family; Miss Lois M. Fawcett of the Minnesota Historical Society for verifying incidents at Pembina; Miss Shirley R. Beresford for drawing the fold-out map; and Mrs. Helen G. Martell for skillfully putting this manuscript into type.

J.E.P.

WEST ON THE 49th PARALLEL

I

TREATIES AND PRELUDES

THE BOUNDARY between Canada and the United
States, where it sweeps westward along the 49th parallel
of north latitude, was once marked by a single oak post,
carved on one side "G.B." and on the other "U.S." But
some humorist among the settlers living in the vicinity of
Red River, or perhaps a passing cynic, uprooted and
turned the post around, so that the "U.S." faced north.
So little did the mark matter, however, that it was allowed
to stand thus until it rotted away.

As late even as 1875 the westernmost settlement in the
Red River Valley was the Métis village of St. Joseph, about
thirty-five miles from Pembina. Beyond that point in the
northern border country not a single permanent habita-
tion existed as far as the Rocky Mountains, if a few Indian
tepees at Turtle Mountain and some log cabins where
half-breeds wintered at Woody Mountain be disregarded.

Much of it arid and treeless, with great extremes of temperature, the land was peopled by roving bands of Sioux, Assiniboine, Blackfeet or Métis hunters who lived off the receding buffalo herds. Through this remote and austere wilderness, a part of the west still unwon, the boundary surveyors of the early 1870's were to make their arduous way.

From the Lake of the Woods to the Pacific Coast the border along the parallel is, between nations, the longest in the world formed by a continuous curve. For many years this 1300-mile line existed only as an imaginary concept, its beginnings going back to the early eighteenth century, when the 49th parallel of north latitude was first suggested to the commissioners under the Treaty of Utrecht as a southern limit for the Hudson's Bay Company in western North America. Although it appeared on several mid-century maps, no such limit was actually fixed by these commissioners, or by subsequent treaty, when Great Britain took over French Canada in 1763 and France ceded Louisiana to Spain.

In diplomatic discussions between the United States and Britain after the Revolution, the point was revived, but the Jay Treaty of 1794 left western boundary questions for settlement by later conventions. Not until the purchase of Louisiana by the United States in 1803 did a division of territory west of the Mississippi River become a live issue. A convention signed in 1806 recognized the 49th parallel as the boundary west of the Lake of the Woods "as far as their said respective territories extend in that quarter," but neither Great Britain nor the United States ratified it.

Initial settlement of the question took place with the

Treaties of 1814 and 1818. The first traced the international line to the Lake of the Woods, it having by then
been discovered that the headwaters of the Mississippi,
named as the western limit in the Treaty of Peace of 1783,
lay south and not west of the lake. The second, for con-
tinuance of the boundary westward, adopted the earlier
suggestion of the 49th parallel of latitude. But the exact
geography of the lake being unknown to them, the treaty
makers specified that from "the most northwestern point
of the Lake" the line should be drawn "due north or south
as the case may be" to the intersection of the 49th parallel,
and then west "along and with" it "to the Stony Mountains." Beyond the mountains the land was left in joint
occupation until the Treaty of 1846 which settled the
Oregon question and fixed the boundary again at 49 degrees north as far as the Strait of Georgia.

Yet this line which may be so simply described as "west
on the 49th parallel" was not as easily marked on the
ground. Perhaps the first attempt to fix its location was
made by the Hudson's Bay Company. In the spring of
1823 it abandoned the fort at Pembina on the Red River,
taken over from the Northwest Company two years
earlier. Astronomical observations had placed the site
too far south to be in British territory. A United States
surveying expedition soon reached the spot, under Major
Stephen H. Long of the Topographical Engineers. His
astronomer, after four days' observations for latitude, determined a point for the parallel as it crossed the Red
River. On the west bank an oak post was forthwith
planted, bearing on its north side "G.B." and on the south
"U.S." This was the mark that some wag later turned
around. Major Long issued a proclamation August 8,

1823, claiming the land south of the post for the United States. Yet neither his action nor that of the Hudson's Bay Company had lasting effect.

The earliest joint act bearing on fixing the line along the 49th parallel was the survey to locate the "most northwestern point of the Lake of the Woods," north or south of which the westward boundary began. This was completed in 1825 by Dr. J.L. Tiarks, acting for the joint commissioners under the Treaty of 1814. He selected the exact point from two possible locations surveyed by David Thompson the year before, but as the point was underwater, no marker could be erected on the spot. Coordinates in latitude and longitude were calculated and measurements made to a reference monument built of logs on firm ground a mile away. Unfortunately the coordinates did not prove reliable nor the monument durable when the initial point for commencing the next survey west was sought almost fifty years later. But Dr. Tiarks' fix did establish conclusively that a due south line would have to be run in order to reach an intersection with the 49th parallel.

Major Long's post on the Red River was renewed substantially in the same place by Captain John Pope, also of the Topographical Engineers, when he visited Pembina in 1850. Meanwhile the Hudson's Bay Company had in 1845 reinstated its fort or store a quarter of a mile to the north, in a position which later observations by Mr. Nicholay, an American scientist, confirmed as being in British territory. When Capt. John Palliser, the British explorer, visited the Hudson's Bay post in 1857, he "adopted" Nicholay's fix, although his own observations brought the 49th parallel 370 yards farther north. This multiplicity of positions may have inspired the citizens of

Pembina to erect in 1860 what became known as the "whiskey post," about a mile north of Long's and Pope's, to stop the smuggling of liquor into the United States from a house near the line. In effect, their action created a no man's land and perhaps opened the door to more serious encroachment ten years later.

Meanwhile settlers from the eastern states, pouring into jointly occupied Oregon territory, brought to a crisis the boundary question on the Pacific coast. Despite political cries of "54-40 or fight" in the Senate, President Polk negotiated a treaty with Great Britain whereby Vancouver Island was left to the latter, and the international boundary extended along the 49th parallel from the crest of the Rocky Mountains to the Strait of Georgia. Due either to the ignorance or obtuseness of the treaty makers, the water boundary between Vancouver Island and the mainland was defined as traversing "the middle of the channel." There were, in fact, several possible channels with the San Juan Islands in between. This oversight in the Treaty of 1846 gave rise to a controversy over national title to the islands not settled until twenty-five years later.

Surveys under the treaty began in 1857, with Archibald Campbell, Chief Clerk of the War Department, appointed United States Commissioner and Lieut. Col. John S. Hawkins of the Royal Engineers, British representative for the land line. For the water boundary there were two separate British Commissioners, Royal Navy Captains James Charles Prevost of H.M.S. *Satellite* and George Henry Richards of H.M.S. *Plumper*. Differences between them and Campbell speedily arose and in 1859, after a company of American troops had taken possession, joint military occupation of the San Juan Islands was agreed upon by the two governments. It continued until

1872 when Kaiser Wilhelm I of Germany sustained the American claim, the issue having been referred to him for arbitration under a clause of the Treaty of Washington of 1871. His decision essentially was that the Canal de Haro, westernmost of the channels and the widest and deepest, rather than Rosario Strait, east of the San Juans, was the one most nearly conforming to the intent of the Treaty of 1846.

A footnote to this award is that when the United States and Great Britain asked to pay the expenses of the arbitration, which the treaty stipulated should be borne equally, the Kaiser declined to submit a bill. Thereupon the American Secretary of State proposed that joint gifts be made to the three German lawyers who had advised the Kaiser. When the Foreign Office, on advice from its minister in Berlin, refrained from participating, Secretary Fish sent over three sets of Audubon's *Birds and Quadrupeds,* in ten volumes each. It perhaps helped assuage British feelings when the German Chancellor, Prince Bismarck, would not allow the lawyers to accept the books.

While the San Juan controversy occupied public attention, the land survey went ahead quietly and co-operatively. Commissioner Campbell was supported by Lieut. John G. Parke of the United States Topographical Engineers as chief astronomer and by a party of civilian surveyors, who entered the field in 1857. Arriving the next year, Colonel Hawkins brought as his chief astronomer Capt. Robert W. Haig, Royal Artillery, assisted by three officers of the Royal Engineers, Capt. Charles J. Darrah, Lieut. Charles W. Wilson and Lieut. Samuel Anderson, the last of whom joined in 1859. The Americans surveyed ninety miles from the coast to the Skagit River in 1858 and 150 miles farther to the Columbia in 1859. Because of the difficulties of a wild and mountainous terrain, particularly in the Cascade Range and the Rockies, the line there was marked only at intervals, astronomical fixes being made in accessible spots where valleys, streams or trails crossed the parallel. Twenty-eight astronomical stations covered a total distance of 409 miles. Eleven were observed by the British, fourteen by the Americans, and three jointly. Where possible, intervening points were established by means of tangent lines between base stations and likewise monumented, with vistas twenty feet wide cut through the forest on either side for half a mile. Altogether 190 miles were thus cleared and marked and a total of 161 monuments erected at intervals varying from one to twenty-five miles.

In one stretch of about sixty-five miles between the Similkameen and the Kettle Rivers, substantial local variations were discovered at five astronomical stations. The Commissioners thereupon agreed to adopt a mean parallel in this section. It was run and marked by Lieutenant Parke in 1861 but the original vistas and demolished cairns remained in place, causing confusion later.

The American and British parties camped and worked separately, the latter wintering the last two years near Fort Colville in Washington Territory and returning to Victoria on Vancouver Island only in the spring of 1862. Both faced formidable problems of organization, transport and supply. To reach the eastern end of the line, the British and some of the Americans used the early steamboat route up the Columbia River to the Dalles, and mule trains overland from there. In the field Indians served them as guides, Mexicans as packers, while occasional dances at Hudson's Bay posts and clashes between gold miners and Indians provided distractions.

Once back at headquarters in Washington or London, map and paper work occupied several years so, with the intervention of the Civil War, it was not until 1869 that the two Commissioners convened in the American capital to sign a final report. Their agreement provided that "between any two successive defined points, marked on the ground, shown on the maps and set forth in the accompanying lists, the line of boundary above described is to be considered a right or straight line," without regard to distances between consecutive points or the course of the parallel in such intervals. This was intended as a practical solution to the problem of fixing the line over impassable ground and of readily determining intermediate points later by local survey, even though it departed from the strict concept of a continuous curve. Although overlooked as a precedent in the next survey, this stipulation ultimately received recognition by treaty all along the parallel.

During the preliminary discussions over the water boundary, Captain Prevost sought to obtain for Great Britain one small piece of mainland that was unquestionably below the 49th parallel, this being Point Roberts. It consisted of a coastal promontory extending about two miles south of the line, having a width somewhat less, and facing the Strait of Georgia on the west and Semiahmoo Bay eastward. A few miles north in British Columbia lay the mouth of the Fraser River, with a growing volume of shipping. Acting on instructions, Captain Prevost proposed that Point Roberts, because of its inaccessibility by land except through British territory, should be left to Great Britain. Commissioner Campbell declined to treat with him on the grounds that the question was one for diplomatic consideration. Accordingly, the

British Minister in Washington brought it up again in
1859 in connection with compromise proposals put forward by Her Majesty's Government for dividing the San
Juan Islands. He was instructed to urge that the Point
had no intrinsic value to either country, although pri-
vately told that American possession would impose a military disadvantage upon British Columbia as well as
trouble from smugglers. But upon failure of the proposed
compromise on San Juan, Point Roberts, however anomalous, remained in the United States.

Altogether, the 1857-61 boundary survey cost the
United States $600,000, or nearly $1,500 a mile, and the
British Government paid out close to £110,000. For
the immediate need this expenditure seems high. The final
report of the American Commissioner as of May 7, 1869,
with those of his chief and assistant astronomers and various scientific annexes was never printed, and the manuscript disappeared from sight a few years later. To this
day it has not been found, although a brief earlier report
by Mr. Campbell and one of Lieutenant Parke's in 1859
were printed. The British Commissioner's final report
embodying the official actions taken by both Commissioners turned up in storage at the Royal Observatory in
Greenwich in 1898 and was printed in Canada a year
later.

Lieut. Samuel Anderson, R.E., who by 1869 had replaced Lieutenant Wilson as Secretary of the British
Commission, came to Washington with Colonel Hawkins
for the final settlement. In a letter home Anderson had
little to say on the boundary business, which went
smoothly, but described instead a reception at the White
House. "Colonel Hawkins and I were introduced by an
old friend, an American naval officer, who seemed in great

favor. In the Reception room we found a crowd of ladies all chattering at the top of their voices, and in the middle of the crowd stood Mrs. Grant supported by two ladies on either side. She received us very graciously and passed us on to a lady on her immediate right. . . . Mrs. Grant was not an attractive [looking] person, about middle-aged, and a decided cast in her eye; her right hand neighbor was most talkative about a recent 'Aurora Borealis' which she said foretold war with England. . . ."

II

ESTIMATES AND PERSONNEL

As PUBLIC opinion in the United States built up pressure for a settlement with England over the Alabama Claims arising from the destruction of Union shipping during the Civil War, clamor among American jingoes for expansion to the north gained new headway. A particular target of the annexationists was Rupert's Land, which the Hudson's Bay Company intended to transfer to the Dominion Government. Its populated part would soon become the province of Manitoba. In neighboring Minnesota the sentiment for acquisition ran particularly strong, its state legislature, even before the Métis uprising of 1869 at Fort Garry, having passed a resolution protesting the transfer to Canada without a vote of the inhabitants. Minnesota's Senator Alexander Ramsey joined Zachariah Chandler of Michigan as an outspoken proponent of annexation. Hence, when a new question arose at the Red River, over the location of the 49th parallel, it aggravated a situation already strained by unrealistic talk and wishful thinking.

That such notions reached high places in the American Government may be seen from the diary of Hamilton Fish, Secretary of State under President Grant. "San Juan being mentioned," he wrote of a discussion in the cabinet, "the President says that he does not care about that, for when the other provinces come to us that will fall with the others. The President evidently expects these provinces to be annexed to the U.S. during his administration. I hope that it may be so. That such is their eventual destiny I doubt not—but whether so soon as the President expects may be a question."

In the winter of 1870 the War Department ordered Gen. George Sykes of the District of Minnesota to survey a new army post at Pembina. He instructed his engineering officer, Capt. David Porter Heap, to mark the position of the parallel at the Red River and the latter, some time during May, took observations. Disregarding the post erected by Major Long in 1823 and renewed by Captain Pope in 1850, Heap made a fix *4,600 feet north* of the previously accepted position and drove stakes west for a distance of thirty-five miles, from the Red River to St. Joseph. Thereupon he departed for Fort Wadsworth in Dakota Territory without filing a report.

As the new line passed well north of the Hudson's Bay Company store, which it will be remembered had since 1845 stood a quarter of a mile above Long's post, the United States Collector of Customs at Pembina, John C. Stoever by name, sprang into action. He descended upon the Hudson's Bay store, took inventory of its stock for the assessment of customs duty, and then, on June 23, wrote the Secretary of the Treasury for instructions. It was from this official that the Secretary of State first learned of the affair. With commendable speed Secretary Fish summoned Sir Edward Thornton, the British Minister in Washington, to give him the bad news. At the latter's request President Grant agreed for the time being to maintain the *status quo* and Stoever was instructed to do nothing further at the Hudson's Bay post, near which a volunteer force of Canadians had since encamped.

Meanwhile Secretary Fish suggested to the British Government that a joint survey of the boundary west of the Lake of the Woods be undertaken to carry out the provisions of the Treaty of 1818. He likewise asked that some Canadian officer verify the recent observations. But Sir Edward Thornton's request for a copy of Captain Heap's report, filed July 9, at St. Paul, was not met, and the report, by curious coincidence, cannot now be found in either War or State Department files. The Washington officials went ahead simply on Stoever's statement of the new position as based on a "series of careful solar and lunar observations." When no specific challenge came from Canada, and since the expediency of joint action seemed quite apparent, the Foreign Office gave tentative approval to Secretary Fish's proposal.

Estimates were obtained by both governments of what it would cost them to survey the boundary from the Lake of the Woods to the summit of the Rockies. General Humphreys, United States Chief of Engineers, figured $100,000 per annum, with a total probable expenditure of $325,000. If engineer officers were assigned, he thought the amount could be revised downward. The British estimate, prepared by Colonel Hawkins with the help of Captain Wilson and Lieutenant Anderson, and reflecting their experience west of the Rockies, came to £100,000. Both estimates contemplated work in the field for three seasons, the British setting forth a detailed operational plan which in the event was quite closely followed. "A good selection of books and games for winter recreation," special seasonal clothing, "breech-loading rifles" and "presents suitable for Indians" were among the requirements. Suggesting a rivalry to come, the specifications for instruments concluded, "It is most undesirable that the results should compare unfavorably with those obtained by the American Commission."

With notable foresight the Royal Engineers officers gave their attention to the "most northwestern point of the Lake of the Woods" and the effect of a due south meridian from it to the 49th parallel. They proposed that the piece of ground on the western shore of the lake which this line would cut off from any land connection with the United States "should, *if possible*, be preserved to the Dominion of Canada." Thus they anticipated the anomaly of what came to be called the Northwest Angle, which, in its inaccessibility from American territory except by water, resembled the promontory at Point Roberts.

President Grant in December, 1870, asked Congress for funds to institute the survey. An appropriation of $100,-000 passed the House by a vote of 120 to 73, but languished in the Senate. Opponents of the bill, Sir Edward Thornton reported, insinuated that it was not worthwhile to take up the question in view of the possibility that the territory north of the boundary might be ceded to the United States as part of a general settlement with Great Britain. Jingoes were still indulging in wishful thinking, with arbitration of the Alabama Claims as yet undecided. In March, 1872, when arbitration under the Treaty of Washington was well under way, Congress appropriated $50,000 for the survey, provided that regular engineer officers of the army were assigned to perform the engineering duties, without any increase in pay.

The need to expedite the survey had become the more obvious as the result of a raid on the Hudson's Bay store at Red River by a group of Fenians the previous October. Led by a self-styled "General" O'Neill whose lieutenants bore such patently Irish names as O'Donohue, Curley and Donnelly, an armed body of men, assembling one morning in Pembina, seized and looted the store. In the absence of Canadian defenders, Capt. Loyd Wheaton, U.S.A., commanding Fort Pembina, proceeded to the scene with two companies of the 20th Infantry. When they deployed, the raiders scattered but were disarmed by Captain Wheaton's men and the ringleaders captured. Seventy-seven breech-loading muskets, eleven sabers, and a few other arms were surrendered, as well as much of the loot. The American force advanced only as far as the line marked by Captain Heap.

When two of the Fenian leaders were charged at St. Paul with conspiracy to violate the neutrality laws, little evidence could be offered of their having plotted in Minnesota. On cross-examination of Captain Wheaton the defense astutely raised the question whether the raid had not actually occurred on United States soil. The Captain testified that he had "never seen the English flag floating over the country where the arrests were made," nor the American flag either. He conceded, "There is some dispute about the jurisdiction of the territory," since no boundary had been established by an international commission. For lack of proof in these respects the prisoners were discharged. This time the Fenians had pulled the British Lion's tail with comparative impunity.

Prior to Congressional action in 1872, the British Government had for a year been ready to proceed with the survey, once the Dominion Government agreed to shoulder half the cost. But following shortly upon this agreement came a nomination from Sir John Macdonald, Prime Minister of Canada, for the post of British Commissioner. His candidate was not a native Canadian but a British officer thirty-seven years of age, Capt. Donald Roderick Cameron of the Royal Artillery. Born in Scotland of old Highland stock, Cameron was educated at French military schools. He secured his army commission in 1856 and served in India after the mutiny. Later as adjutant of the artillery he took part in the Bhootan campaign of 1864-65, for which he received mention in dispatches. Posted to Halifax soon after, he married in 1869 Emma, the daughter of Dr. Charles Tupper, ex-Premier of Nova Scotia and a member of Sir John Macdonald's cabinet. During the winter of 1871 Cameron gained attention at Ottawa by saving a man from drowning in the Rideau Canal. For this rescue in icy water he received the Bronze Medal of the Royal Humane Society.

Sir John's candidate had also been aide-de-camp to Lieutenant Governor William McDougall of Manitoba, who during the Red River uprising of 1869 was prevented from reaching his post by the Métis supporters of Louis Riel. Cameron himself was turned back from a barricade on the way to Fort Garry, while affording its defenders much amusement by examining it through a monocle. In the course of his western sojourn the captain came to know the renowned Bishop Taché of St. Boniface and translated from the French the latter's *Sketch of the North-West of America*. In it there is quoted this revealing comment, made to the bishop by a British admirer of the Blackfeet: "The Blackfeet are to other Indians what the English are to other people."

After querying his military superiors, the Foreign Office assented to the appointment of Captain Cameron as Commissioner, although an officer of the Royal Engineers would have been preferred. But Colonel Hawkins did not wish the appointment, Captain Wilson had recently become chief of the topographical department of the War Office, and Anderson was still a lieutenant. The naming of the engineering staff for the survey was referred to the War Office, which selected Anderson for chief astronomer, and Albany Featherstonhaugh, an engineer officer slightly junior to Anderson, as his first assistant. Both were promoted to captain August 8, 1872.

Samuel Anderson was born November 15, 1839, in London, the son of another Samuel Anderson, an official in the High Court of Chancery. He was educated in Scotland at St. Andrews University and the Military Academy at Edinburgh, before being selected for the Royal Military Academy. Entering at Woolwich in August, 1857, he won a prize sword for exemplary conduct and was gazetted a lieutenant in the Royal Engineers December 21, 1858. His first foreign service was in the Pacific northwest, from 1859 to 1862 as already noted. Soon after the London map work for that survey ended in 1864, Anderson was selected to go with Captain Wilson to Syria to survey and map the Holy Land, under the sponsorship of the Palestine Exploration Fund, returning after a year. From 1866 to 1871 he held a teaching appointment at the School of Military Engineering, Chatham, and it was during this period that he visited Washington in company with Colonel Hawkins. He also attended the Prussian army maneuvers at Königsberg in September, 1869. At an early age Anderson acquired a reputation for thoroughness as well as tact and amiability.

The man named assistant astronomer was a son of George William Featherstonhaugh, the distinguished explorer, geologist and lecturer, who acted as the British Commissioner in the Maine-Quebec border survey of 1840 and traveled extensively in western America before becoming British Consul at Havre in 1844. His son Albany was the issue of a second marriage to Charlotte Carter, by birth a Virginian and the daughter of a half-sister of Robert E. Lee. Albany's connection with the Confederate general was somewhat remote, for his grandmother was twenty years older than Marse Robert. Yet it undoubtedly served the great-nephew in good stead when in November, 1864, he ran the blockade from Bermuda to visit Richmond and observe the Confederate defenses before Petersburg.

The result of this visit was a professional paper that appeared in the Royal Engineers yearbook shortly after the close of the war. It relates one stratagem which Featherstonhaugh himself probably witnessed: Between Colquitt's and Gracie's salients at Petersburg the Federals maintained a picket line on rising ground before a ravine, through which a brook ran into the Confederate lines and on to the Appomattox River. Downstream, out of sight of the pickets, the Confederates built a dam across the ravine, leaving sluice gates so the brook ran as before. On the night of a heavy rain the gates were shut and the rising water flooded the ground behind the Federal pickets. At daybreak the Confederates attacked and in the confusion created by the flood succeeded in breaking up the outpost and capturing a number of prisoners. Thereafter, the Federals did not replace the pickets so, the observer noted, "the defense of that portion of the line was rendered much easier."

Featherstonhaugh, born September 6, 1840, took prizes in mathematics and languages at his schools in Wimbledon and Bath, before attending the Royal Military Academy at Woolwich. He was gazetted lieutenant in the Royal Engineers June 22, 1859, Bermuda being his first foreign station, then Halifax in alternate years from 1867 to 1870. There he met Captain Cameron, who in fact suggested him for chief astronomer and as an alternate choice for secretary to the Commission. At the time of the selection Featherstonhaugh was, like Anderson, teaching at Chatham. He was professionally able and quite tireless. No doubt from growing up at Havre he could speak French, but one of his relatives found him reticent to the point of being monosyllabic.

Cameron's first choice for secretary was Lieut. Arthur Clitheroe Ward, R.E., who received the appointment. Commissioned from Woolwich in 1860, he had been stationed in Nova Scotia from 1865 to 1870 and had known Cameron there. Ward was methodical in office work and got on well with his fellows. The junior officer appointed as assistant astronomer, Lieut. William James Galwey, R.E., came from Mallow, County Cork, Ireland. He was born there in 1841, the same year as Ward. Galwey received his commission from Woolwich in 1862 and like Featherstonhaugh and Ward saw service in Nova Scotia between 1867 and 1870. His letters reveal him as inclined to take a dim view of things, but nonetheless a man of humor.

None of these officers on the British Commission were married, except Captain Cameron. In addition to military pay, which for a captain was only £200 a year and for a lieutenant £140, the survey pay was set at £1,000 per annum for the Commissioner, £600 for the chief astronomer, £400 for his assistants and £350 for the secretary. They also received advances of £100 each for equipment, besides traveling expenses and rations. Thus in contrast to assigned U.S. engineer officers, barred by Congressional proviso from receiving extra compensation, the Royal Engineers were well off. Archibald Campbell, as the American Commissioner, received a salary of $4,000 per annum and six dollars a day in commutation of expenses. He was appointed to this new boundary assignment in June, 1872, and instructed to organize a party for the survey. The Chief of Engineers detailed Brevet Lieut. Col. Francis U. Farquhar as chief astronomer, and Brevet Maj. William J. Twining, Capt. James F. Gregory and Lieut. Francis Vinton Greene as assistants.

Campbell himself was not without engineering experience. He had graduated from West Point in 1835 but resigned from the army after a year's frontier duty in Louisiana. For some years thereafter he worked as a civil engineer on various railway, canal and river surveys in the south and east of the United States until becoming, in 1844, private secretary to the Secretary of War, William L. Marcy. This led to his appointment as Chief Clerk of the War Department two years later. Of Scottish ancestry like both Cameron and Anderson, Campbell was the son of another Archibald who for forty years served as Deputy Secretary of State of the State of New York and President of the St. Andrews Society. Born in 1813, the United

States Boundary Commissioner was over twenty years senior to his opposite number Captain Cameron, with long experience in handling the kinds of problem likely to confront them.

III

THE COMMISSIONS REACH PEMBINA

THE TWO Commissioners first met in Washington in July, 1872, where they agreed to start work at Pembina. Captain Cameron had taken Ward with him as secretary, leaving Anderson to complete the organization of the survey party in England. In self-preparation the junior engineer officers, Featherstonhaugh and Galwey, took refresher courses in astronomy at the Royal Observatory in Greenwich, while Anderson busied himself gathering together instruments and equipment and selecting the contingent of forty-four noncommissioned officers and men of the Royal Engineers who were to go on the expedition. Their ranks consisted of a sergeant major, a quartermaster sergeant, two sergeants, four corporals, four second corporals, five lance corporals, and twenty-seven sappers, representing among them the trades of blacksmith, wheelwright, carpenter, mason, surveyor, saddler, baker, shoemaker, tailor, clerk and photographer. The capabilities and discipline of these men, who like the officers were to receive extra "boundary pay," would add immeasurably to the effectiveness of the British party.

The memorandum of instructions that Captain Cameron left behind him (it was the first of many) charged Lieutenant Featherstonhaugh with the duty of procuring a field library, to include stationery and indoor games. An inventory of the several hundred volumes he chose lists three copies each of Galton's *Art of Travel, At Home in the Wilderness,* and *Shifts of Camp Life.* Most numerous were the works of fiction, history, essays, plays and poetry by such authors as Dickens, Dumas, Fielding, Scott, Trollope, Sterne, Smollett, Swift, Carlyle, Thackeray, Macaulay, Milton, Shakespeare, Byron, Wordsworth, Hood and Pope. American authors found representation in Cooper, Hawthorne, Holmes, Prescott, Poe, Bret Harte and Artemas Ward.

The library also contained a sprinkling of sporting books, like Frank Forrester's *Fish and Fishing,* Wright's *Gun, Rod and Saddle, Sponge's Sporting Tour* and *Stonehenge on Shooting,* and such clearly relevant titles as *Red River Expedition, Roughing it in the Bush,* and *North West Passage by Land.* Two volumes on Waterloo, Creasy's *Fifteen Decisive Battles of the World* and Napier's *Peninsular War* represented the military field, while natural history, mountaineering and arctic exploration likewise had their exemplars. All these volumes were required to be packed in units of less than a hundred pounds for easy carriage on the backs of men or animals.

From Washington Captain Cameron hastened to Ottawa to confer with the Surveyor General over the appointment of a civilian staff of surveyors and other Canadian aides. The two principal surveying posts were filled by Lieut. Col. A.G. Forrest of the Canadian Militia, a Provincial Land Surveyor, and Alexander Lindsay Russell, Deputy Surveyor General. The Dominion Government likewise nominated as subassistant astronomers Messrs. George F. Burpee, William F. King, William A. Ashe and George C. Coster, who all participated in three seasons of work. The post of commissary went to Lawrence W. Herchmer, a former ensign in the 46th Regiment of Foot, who after service in India came to Canada and married the daughter of a late member of the Provincial Parliament from Toronto. Herchmer had been born in England in 1840. Dr. T.J.W. Burgess of Toronto was appointed surgeon, with Dr. Thomas Millman, a young man just out of medical school, as assistant. George Mercer Dawson, another young man who was the son of the principal of McGill College in Montreal, served as naturalist and geologist, and Dr. William George Boswell as veterinarian.

Each of the above, as well as several assistants to the surveyors later named, ranked as an officer of the British Commission, and received the same allowance for outfit as the Royal Engineers. Their pay was $2,000 per annum for the commissary, surgeon and geologist, $1,800 for the surveyors, $1,750 for the veterinary and $1,500 for the subassistant astronomers. That some, at least, of these appointments were regarded as political patronage may be inferred from a letter of thanks from Lawrence Herchmer to Alexander Campbell, a member of the Dominion Cabinet from Ontario and Conservative leader of the Senate. The commissary wrote of having enjoyed his "berth long enough to form a pretty fair estimate of its value" and ended, "I am afraid our appointments will not be worth much to us after two years," when he suggested, "unless some friendly Indian interposes . . . a grateful country may have an opportunity of reemploying our services."

Captain Cameron's instructions from the Foreign Office defined his task as the "scientific ascertainment of a fixed geographical line," to be regarded as "a question of fact not depending upon opinion or argument." He was told that a variation of the line to eliminate the Northwest Angle did not come within the province of the Commissioners, but was to be negotiated between the two governments. The Foreign Office wanted a survey first, with discussion of modifications kept within its own control. This program of course reflected the confidential recommendation of Colonel Hawkins that the isolated piece of land on the western shore of the Lake of the Woods be preserved, *if possible,* to Canada. When Captain Cameron reported from Ottawa certain doubts expressed by the American Commissioner at their initial conference as to the position of the "most northwestern point" of the Lake, due to the lack of a monument or correct co-ordinates, he was again advised that any discussion was premature until the facts were ascertained by survey and the Commissioners had agreed on a map. Thus it appears that both Commissioners were quite aware, before they reached the spot, that finding its exact location might prove difficult.

While Cameron and Ward were occupied in Ottawa and other Canadian cities making arrangements for personnel and supplies, Archibald Campbell dispatched three of his engineer officers and their civilian assistants to St. Paul, Minnesota, to make preparations for the field. Lieutenant Greene was sent on ahead with thirty-two boxes of surveying instruments to Fort Pembina, where he arrived with Lewis Boss, assistant astronomer, August 17. A train of wagons, horses and mules was provided by the Quartermaster General to convey the American Commission and their tents, rations and forage to Pembina from Fort Abercrombie, a military post accessible from St. Paul by railroad. Second Lieut. O.D. Ladley, 22nd Infantry, had charge of the train and served thenceforth as quartermaster and commissary for the commission. Commissioner Campbell having reached St. Paul, the party proceeded to Fort Abercrombie, whence they arrived at Fort Pembina, September 5, after a march of eight days. There they found waiting for them Company K of the 20th Infantry, assigned as escort, under the command of Capt. Abram A. Harbach. With commendable tact and perhaps guided by Lieutenant Greene, who had already taken preliminary observations, the American Commissioner pitched camp two days later on the west bank of the Red River near the post set up by Major Long and renewed by Captain Pope, to await the arrival of the British party. At this point the Red River was about seventy-five yards wide, with a depth of ten feet in the center. It flowed north with a normal current of two and a half miles an hour, low water level being thirty-four feet below the adjacent prairie.

Meanwhile Samuel Anderson, now promoted to captain, embarked his contingent of Royal Engineers, August 22, at Liverpool aboard the *Scandinavian* for Quebec. From England he brought with him all the astronomical instruments, besides chronometers borrowed from the Royal Navy, a Royal Engineers photographic outfit and Adams breech-loading revolvers for his officers and men. When the War Office insisted on charging Anderson with personal liability for the return of the fire-

arms, the Foreign Office was induced to notify Captain
Cameron that the responsibility would be his, once Anderson had joined. As special stores the English party also
took along a supply of compressed vegetables and Liebig's
extract of meat.

Landing at Quebec, September 1, Captain Anderson
met and was invited to dine with the Governor General,
Lord Dufferin, himself a former Royal Engineer. Captain Featherstonhaugh received an invitation also. Anderson found Lord Dufferin "most agreeable and affable."
His wife, Lady Dufferin, "looks about twenty, is very
pretty, and is full of conversation." The next day the survey party took a river steamer to Montreal, and from there
a lake boat to Kingston and Toronto, passing by canal
around the Lachine Rapids in the St. Lawrence River,
and through the Thousand Islands.

At Kingston on September 6, the two captains left Lieutenant Galwey on board with the men and twenty tons
of freight, themselves proceeding ahead on the Grand
Trunk railway. After a night in billets at Toronto where
the officers, according to Galwey, had a very good dinner
and "a parting from civilization in the shape of Moselle,"
the whole group went by train to Collingwood on
Georgian Bay, where Captain Anderson organized a lake-
shore bathing party. Thence a steamer took them in four
days through Lakes Huron and Superior to Duluth, Minnesota. Captain Cameron and his wife and baby were met
with here and arrangements made to proceed by train to
Moorhead on the Red River, then the nearest point to
Pembina on the Northern Pacific Railway. Transit of the
Royal Engineers and their supplies through United
States territory had already been sanctioned in Washington.

At Moorhead the baggage was loaded into wagons drawn by ox-teams and a three-day march begun by road to Frog Point, at that time of year the head of navigation on the Red River, even for light draft steamers. At this place, below Goose Rapids, the river was about forty-five yards wide and four feet deep. Here Captain Anderson and most of the party boarded the *Dakota* of the Kittson line, and after several days of tortuous navigation which, as Lieutenant Galwey commented, "would puzzle an R.N.," this small sternwheeler arrived at North Pembina early in the morning of September 18. The Royal Engineers encamped about four hundred yards from the Americans and not far from the Hudson's Bay store.

Captain Anderson found the British Commissioner, who had come overland from Frog Point two days earlier, much preoccupied with his family, for whom no suitable accommodation in the vicinity could be discovered. After but half an hour's conference with the American Commissioner, Captain Cameron hurried off to board the waiting steamer and proceed downstream to Fort Garry. There he intended to lodge his wife and baby with friends. Fortunately Captain Anderson from the previous survey was well known and congenial to Mr. Campbell. But the precipitate departure of Captain Cameron left the British chief astronomer to bear the burden of organization alone.

The brief meeting of September 18 between the two Commissioners and their chief astronomers decided that the first order of business was to fix the parallel on the western bank of the Red River by joint observations. It was agreed then to run the boundary eastward to its intersection with the due south line from the "most northwestern point" of the Lake of the Woods, which, with the point where the parallel touched the lake, should also be jointly determined. Intermediate points on the line eastward of Red River were to be alternately observed. This work was expected to occupy the balance of the season of 1872, and while the astronomers were so occupied, the surveyors of each party were to map a five-mile belt of country on their respective sides of the parallel. During the winter, when the Americans expected to retire from the field to Detroit, the British would cut out a vista thirty feet wide along the established boundary, at the joint expense of the two commissions.

Major Twining who had already begun a series of observations for latitude at the Red River, was succeeded on station by Captain Featherstonhaugh. Their final results, quite separately arrived at, differed by only thirty-two feet. The difference was halved to reach a fix acceptable to both Commissioners. It confirmed that the Hudson's Bay Company store stood north of the parallel, although only one hundred yards from it instead of a quarter of a mile. The Canadian custom house was found to be 540 feet inside American territory. The true location of these buildings was nowhere noted in the published reports of either Commissioner, which seems strange, since this question ostensibly gave rise to the whole survey. Yet it is no stranger than the inexplicability of Captain Heap's error, which received no mention either. In those days a series of observations on land with no more elaborate instrument than a sextant could be expected to fix latitude accurately within a hundred yards. Perhaps the Commissioners' desire was to let sleeping dogs lie, while dealing with what seemed to them more weighty problems.

IV

AT THE NORTHWEST POINT

Both COMMISSIONS had no sooner become settled in camp at North Pembina than there began on September 22 a severe equinoctial gale which lasted nearly four days. Snow fell for forty-eight hours, and there was a marked drop in temperature, disrupting activities outside the tents. The storm was preceded and its coming announced by large flocks of wild geese flying south over the Red River.

Yet three weeks of fine weather ensued, enabling the survey parties to get well started, and construction of British winter quarters at Dufferin, the new name for North Pembina, to be commenced. These consisted of several wooden frame buildings designed by Lieutenant Ward, of which a two-story structure with offices and a messroom and kitchen below, and bedrooms above, was the most conspicuous. With accommodations for twelve officers of the Commission, Lieutenant Galwey found it a "perfect palace." Three other buildings provided barracks and mess facilities for eighty men, and there were besides a storehouse, cookhouse, bakery, workshop and a stable for thirty horses. The whole construction, including a separate house for Captain Cameron, was finished, November 13, at a cost of £6,000, by a contractor who obtained most of his building materials and labor from Minnesota.

Captain Cameron returned from Fort Garry ahead of the storm, in time to hear from Mr. Russell, who since the beginning of September had been scouting the lay of the land at the Lake of the Woods. His report suggested further complications there in that the meandering channel line to the "most northwestern point" of the lake and a due south line therefrom would probably cross each other. In forwarding this information to the Foreign Office, the British Commissioner wrote he had not communicated with Commissioner Campbell on the subject, since the Americans' own discovery of the "loop" might help achieve the desired readjustment at the Northwest Angle.

But Archibald Campbell's attention had already fastened on another subject. While his fellow commissioner was writing to London, he was supplying Washington with an appraisal of the other team. "The British Commission have come out fully prepared to keep two observing parties in the field," he wrote to Secretary Fish, "while the United States Commission with its present limited means can have only one. The British Commission are in every respect better provided than the United States Commission. Their instruments are new and of the best quality while most of ours are old and somewhat dilapidated.

. . . Their detachment of sappers alone gives them a great advantage over us by having a disciplined body of men regularly trained to fulfil the subordinate duties required by the Commission, and at a moderate expense, compared with the employment of persons in civil life qualified for similar duties." Hampered by the niggardliness of the initial appropriation, Campbell was determined to get more out of Congress another time.

This report preceded by a few days an estimate of expenses amounting to $125,000 for the ensuing fiscal year and a statement, which Campbell induced Cameron to give him, of the superior organization and funds of the British. Captain Cameron took evident satisfaction in writing that with four officers, forty-four Royal Engineers and forty-two civilians, not to speak of additional temporary employees, he could put in the field three astronomical parties, two for surveying, four for depots and one for headquarters. He gave the payroll of his staff and estimated a total expenditure of £100,000 over three years, as to which, he said, "I have been honored by having confidence reposed in my discretion." In empire building the two Commissioners unquestionably saw eye to eye, and their relations were never more cordial.

The honeymoon did not survive their joint visit to the Lake of the Woods, undertaken in October by way of Fort Garry and the emigrant route to Manitoba known as the Dawson Road. Preceding the Commissioners by about ten days, the two chief astronomers arrived at the lake to search for the remains of the reference monument built by David Thompson in 1824 to mark the "most northwestern point" selected by Dr. Tiarks the following year. It was described as a pyramid of logs, twelve feet high by six and a half on a side, the lower logs oak and the upper

Dr. Thomas Millman UPPER LEFT

Lieut. Francis V. Greene, U. S. Engs. UPPER RIGHT

Capt. Samuel Anderson, R. E. LOWER LEFT

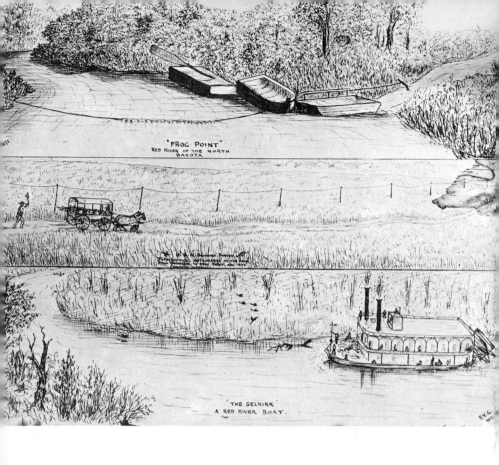

"FROG POINT"
RED RIVER OF THE NORTH
DAKOTA

"THE SELKIRK"
A RED RIVER BOAT.

Sketches by Lieut. Greene, 1872
New York Public Library

Steamer *Selkirk* at Dufferin
Pub. Archives Canada

British Boundary Commission
Lieut. Galwey, Capt. Ward, Comm'r Cameron,
Capt. Featherstonhaugh, Dr. Burgess,
Dr. Boswell SEATED L. TO R.
Burpee, King, Coster, Herchmer, Capt. Anderson,
Dr. Dawson, Russell, Ashe STANDING

Barracks at Dufferin UPPER RIGHT

Fort Pembina, Dakota Territory LOWER RIGHT

Millman

The "Most Northwestern Point," marked by white post beyond
canoe UPPER LEFT

Royal Engineers Detachment LOWER LEFT
Capt. Anderson, Capt. Featherstonhaugh FRONT CENTER
Capt. Ward, Lieut. Galwey FRONT RIGHT

Pub. Archives Canada

Rebuilt Reference Monument, Northwest Angle UPPER RIGHT
Dr. Dawson holding gun

The Due South Line, Northwest Angle OVERLEAF

Int. Boundary Comm.

part aspen. The astronomers had no difficulty in finding the northwestern arm of the lake, which near its extremity had a channel less than a hundred yards wide, but there was no sign of the monument. A rise in the water level of the lake, winter ice, or forest fire may have caused its disappearance. After three days' futile search, during which the local Ojibway Indians proved less than helpful, James McKay, a mixed-blood member of the Manitoba legislature and the manager of the Dawson Road, induced an ancient chief to point out the site. His directions led to a spot on the marshy shore where, among some rushes in two feet of water, the remains of a square crib of logs were found. One of them, hand-hewn and charred, was dredged up and turned out to be six feet long and of oak.

The two chief astronomers rejoiced that their search had ended before the advent of the Commissioners. When the stated courses and distances were run from the site indicated by the old Indian, the "most northwestern point" of the lake appeared to be fifteen hundred yards away, very close to the end of the arm and within five hundred feet of the latitude given by Dr. Tiarks, although his longitude was nearly five miles out. Yet on the arrival of the Commissioners from Fort Garry a day or so later, all was confusion again. Commissioner Campbell was quite satisfied with the evidence of the monument but Captain Cameron refused to accept it as conclusive. He took his instructions to avoid discussion most literally and felt justified in referring the circumstances to his Government for decision. No doubt he hoped that a postponement might in some way help to save the Northwest Angle for Canada.

The British Commissioner took refuge in the fact that the reference monument was described as standing on the "nearest firm ground" to the northwest point, whereas a granite outcrop appeared much nearer than the site accepted by the astronomers. This evasiveness on the part of his chief mortified and embarrassed Captain Anderson, who had found Colonel Farquhar friendly and co-operative and wished to reciprocate. On October 24, he wrote confidentially to his mother from the Lake of the Woods: "Our work was getting on swimmingly, the Americans and ourselves working hand in hand, till the American and our own Commissioner arrived four days ago, when *our* representative created some difficulties which will cause the United States party and my own a fortnight's more labour at this place in taking an elaborate series of observations, all for nothing. . . . Our Commissioner has so far neither turned out brilliant nor successful. He has a most unfortunate habit of rubbing everybody the wrong way without meaning anything. Poor Mr. Campbell, the American Commissioner, is terribly put out . . ."

In a later letter, written after the Commissioners had left the scene, Anderson expressed his feelings even more pointedly: "Colonel Farquhar, the United States Chief Astronomer, is very genial and amusing. We are in perfect accord with regard to the work. One night when the knotty question of the identification of the monument was before the Commissioners he was heard to start up in his sleep and exclaim: 'Any fool could tell *that* was a monument!' One of his own officers who occupied the same tent heard it and tells the story with great gusto."

Captain Cameron's refusal to recognize the site of the monument, and thus fix the place of commencement for the due south line, was not the only irritant in his relations with Commissioner Campbell. Just before setting out for the Lake of the Woods they had dined together in camp at North Pembina. There the American Commissioner casually mentioned that his cook, an ex-soldier by the name of James Brady, was a Fenian. Cameron, on ascertaining that the man had participated in the raid of the previous fall on the Hudson's Bay Company store, took it upon himself to advise Campbell to leave the cook behind on their journey. His explanation was that Brady might himself be attacked by anti-Fenian Britishers while passing through Manitoba. "Mr. Campbell—to my astonishment—immediately flared into stars and stripes," so the British Commissioner wrote, and wished to put to the test whether "any one dared to interfere with a man under his official protection." However, after sleeping on it, Campbell changed his mind and consented to share Cameron's cook on the trip. When they returned to North Pembina, November 6, Brady was in custody on the American side, awaiting trial on a charge of highway robbery with violence.

This story was told by Captain Cameron himself in private correspondence with an official of the Foreign Office, to indicate the writer's tact in dealing with the American Commissioner. In the same letter the captain exculpated himself for the failure to agree at the Lake of the Woods. As he interpreted it: "Mr. Campbell tried to persuade me that my duty was to determine and mark the N.W. Point itself: and on my declining to accept his views, attacked the scope of my Commission." In reality, the American Commissioner was far more discerning. As his report shows, he was well aware of Cameron's policy and objective—to leave the question of the "most northwestern point" unsettled, and hence the ownership of the Northwest Angle in abeyance. In this bit of land a depot and steamboat landing had already been built at the lake end of the Fort Garry road, which was then the only all-Canadian route to Manitoba from the eastern provinces.

Captain Cameron's delaying tactics were all the more apparent since he had no alternative of his own for the establishment of the "most northwestern point." He did, moreover, agree to the cutting of a sight line due south from the point recommended by the two chief astronomers, through sixteen miles of timber to the shore of the lake, without, however, accepting it as part of the boundary. This was in fact accomplished by a British party of axmen and Indians under the direction of Captain Anderson, after the Americans had withdrawn for the winter. Meanwhile Major Twining and Lieutenant Galwey made joint observations to fix the 49th parallel on the west shore of the Lake of the Woods, a task they completed in October with a difference of only twenty-nine feet in their independent results. The spot was located and marked on a sand spit near Buffalo Point. Eastward along the parallel from Red River Lieutenant Greene surveyed thirty-three miles to the Roseau River. Lientenant Galwey fixed the parallel twenty miles east at West Roseau and Captain Featherstonhaugh thirty-six miles farther near Pine River. These astronomical stations were chosen because of firm ground in an otherwise swampy terrain.

The seeds of dissension between the Commissioners, sown during their trip to the Lake of the Woods, flourished immediately on their return to North Pembina. Commissioner Campbell took precipitate leave of his opposite number to go to his own camp, where he was undoubtedly cheered by the news that the Kaiser had on October 21 decided the San Juan arbitration in favor of the United States. His anxiety over it and "exultation at the result" were noted by Captain Cameron. After a couple of days in camp the latter ran into the American Commissioner making purchases at the Hudson's Bay store, only to learn that Campbell and his chief astronomer intended leaving Pembina for the winter that very evening. When the British Commissioner hurriedly sought to get official confirmation of the exact fix of the parallel at the Red River, he was put off with the excuse that the American astronomical calculations had not been fully worked. Two could play at the waiting game, and henceforth relations between the Commissioners would be formal, if not frigid.

V

WINTER WORK

NAVIGATION on the Red River closed November 12, 1872, when the stream froze over. With the departure on the same day of Captain Gregory, Lieutenant Greene, their trains and escort for Fort Abercrombie, to be followed shortly by Major Twining, only the British Commission remained at the boundary, now comfortably housed in permanent quarters at Dufferin. All three British astronomical parties continued in the field—Captain Anderson at the Northwest Angle, and Featherstonhaugh and Galwey observing at different points along the parallel eastward of Red River.

Each of the officers had encounters with Indians, Ojibway or Chippewa, living in the vicinity of the Lake of the Woods. These inhabitants were inquisitive and suppliant, rather than hostile. At Buffalo Point while camping with Major Twining, Lieutenant Galwey "was pestered by the

Indian Chief who came attended by his braves and his
father, a fine looking old man over a hundred years old."
Two lengthy palavers endured by both officers caused
Galwey to observe that the Indians "in their speeches are
very like Englishmen. They commence by saying they are
not much of a hand at talking and then jaw away over two
hours." The speakers all ended by saying they were very
hungry, "which I had to appease with pork."

In cutting out the due south line Captain Anderson
employed a dozen Chippewa axmen, whom he found lack-
ing in stamina and difficult to keep steadily at work, but
far better toters than his own men. Each morning began
with a parley over pay or food. Concessions in provisions
were often made, so that the camp was soon surrounded
by wives, children and old people. Standard daily rations
were 1½ lbs. of salt pork, 2½ lbs. of flour and 1 oz. of tea
per laborer. The chief astronomer was visited at his tent
by one persistent pair to whom he gave some tobacco.
This did not satisfy as they had been told he had come
there "to give out food to the Indians." Another native,
shrewdly calling himself the American Chief, visited
Colonel Farquhar to ask for food and clothing. His only
reward after a long speech was to be told, "Noble Red
Brother, I will tell your story to the Great White Father
in Washington!"

On the Dawson Road Captain Anderson met a white
man tramping along from the direction of Fort Garry. He
turned out to be an Irishman, and though immediately
suspected of being a Fenian, was permitted to accompany
the party for a day or so and mess with the men. Another
encounter was with an individual calling himself "Lord"
Gordon, who appeared at the Lake of the Woods in the
guise of a traveler of means and a sportsman possessing a

wonderful stock of guns. But Anderson was repelled by
his familiarity and suspicious when "Lord" Gordon spent
all his time cooking and never went shooting. The de-
nouement came when a newspaper found its way into
camp with the report that Gordon was a notorious swin-
dler and bail jumper wanted by the New York police. He
was subsequently seized near Winnipeg by two American
detectives but liberated before they could take him across
the border at Pembina. Instead the kidnapers were jailed
and tried in Canada, although ultimately released after
pleading guilty because their arrest took place just south
of the newly fixed boundary.

Captain Anderson found the ground at the Northwest
Angle very swampy, and covered with a tangle of fallen
trees and blowdowns. In places devoid of timber a mossy
surface gave way underfoot into bog and water. At the
north end of the cutting there were dense stands of birch,
tamarack and larch, thinning out and becoming stunted
as the line struck a marsh at the edge of the lake. With the
help of the Indians the cutting was completed, November
21, just as freezing temperatures made the surface less
treacherous. The British chief astronomer, his observations finished at the northwest point, supervised the last
few miles and erected a flagpole in the ice at the lake shore
during a gale. Sounding the spot in the lake where the
due south line intersected the parallel, he noted a depth
of thirty feet. Anderson returned to Fort Garry in three
days, during which the thermometer went to 30 degrees
below zero. From there he wrote home with marked re-
straint: "I should like the old Plenipotentiaries who decided this Boundary Line by Treaty in 1818 to be resusci-
tated for a short time, in order to come and live at this
spot. They would probably have then decided to fix it in

some other locality, instead of a swamp, where it will be difficult to find a spot for setting up a permanent mark."

The telegraph line having just reached Fort Garry, Captain Anderson found an urgent summons from the British Commissioner, as well as a message from Mr. Russell in Chicago that he was ready to exchange time signals for longitude. The last took precedence, so over nine hundred miles of wire the chief astronomer checked chronometers with the Chicago Observatory by instantaneous messages. The next day in very cold weather he drove sixty-five miles by stage to the Hudson's Bay Company store in North Pembina, where he found Captain and Mrs. Cameron, the lady unfortunately suffering from frostbite on her cheek. In succeeding nights at the beginning of December more telegraphic signals were exchanged with Chicago, while Lieutenant Galwey observed the stars outside to fix the time. As a result the longitude at Red River was established with a probable error of less than a hundred yards.

Lieutenant Galwey had returned to headquarters at Dufferin on November 19, after fixing the parallel twenty miles east on a ridge at West Roseau. His observations were made in below zero weather with oil freezing in the lamps of his instruments. Going to bed in the extreme cold, he lit his pipe, took off his moccasins and undressed under the blankets, reversing the process getting up. Overcoming the habits of a lifetime, he "put the bath in the corner of the tent. Look at it but do no more."

Galwey gave his men the same Spartan treatment. To one of them complaining of indigestion, the lieutenant administered three strong pills. Since the patient was no better when Lieutenant Greene's party happened by, Galwey sent him to the American doctor. The man neglected to mention the original dose, so received another one exactly the same. Galwey quoted him as saying that later on he felt much better, but that "the remedy was very violent." Another time, to relieve a steady diet of salt pork, Galwey issued a bottle of lime juice, telling his corporal to give every man a drink of it. "Suddenly I heard very bad language and saw a man rushing for the lake and commencing to drink. It turned out the lime juice was concentrated and ought to have been mixed with six times its own amount of water. After this I could get nobody to take it."

Captain Featherstonhaugh remained out in camp from the end of October, first at Pine River fixing the parallel, and then running and cutting out survey lines from that point toward Red River. On December 21, Captain Anderson found him "in wonderfully good spirits" near Point d'Orme. The chief astronomer had left Dufferin with Commissary Herchmer to see how the field parties were getting on. In spite of the intense cold Captain Featherstonhaugh was loath to suspend the work, which progressed readily over the frozen swamps and muskeg. It was therefore decided to establish two provision depots in log cabins, one thirty-three miles from Red River at Point d'Orme on the Roseau River, and another about sixty miles away at Pine River. After helping his assistant astronomer move camp, Captain Anderson returned to Dufferin by sleigh, during a night when the thermometer registered 51 degrees below zero. With Featherstonhaugh he left two turkeys and a supply of currants, raisins and suet for a Christmas plum pudding. The turkeys could only be cooked in pieces, but the pudding with rum sauce was a great success.

After church parade conducted by Captain Anderson,

Christmas Day, 1872, at Dufferin was celebrated by shaking hands with visiting Indians and drinking champagne at dinner. Lieutenant Galwey noted that he received no "X-mas boxes and gave none." The commissary had his nose frostbitten four times in the morning and as a last resort "had it put into a bag." With other staff members Anderson paid a call on the American officers at Fort Pembina. They were warmly received by the commander, Capt. Loyd Wheaton, whose wife was the only lady at the post. Visiting other quarters in turn and taking refreshments in each became quite strenuous. Dr. Burgess developed a headache and on arriving home went supperless to bed. He insisted on taking six quinine pills which were hesitantly brought him, whereas a request for extra covers resulted in a mound being built on his bed, topped off by a portable bathtub.

At New Year's Eve came the men's turn to celebrate. A dance was organized, with two fiddlers, and all the Métis neighbors were invited. Captain Cameron headed the subscription list with a contribution of £2. Captain Anderson thought the party a success but according to Lieutenant Galwey, "only three of the women kind came. But all of the male sex appeared who all got drunk, so they have abandoned the idea of any more assemblies."

On the first day of 1873 the indefatigable chief astronomer set out on another trip to the line, this time to supply the new depots and to get in touch with outlying survey parties. Captain Featherstonhaugh's camp was reached in one day, but it took four days more through deep unbroken snow for the sleighs to arrive at the furthest depot, ninety miles roundabout from Pembina. There Captain Anderson found two men with a dog team from Colonel Forrest's party, which since November had been surveying the shores of the Lake of the Woods while drawing supplies via the Dawson Road. Deciding to rest his horses and teamster at the Pine River depot, the chief astronomer with one other man took to snowshoes and followed the two voyageurs and their dog-drawn toboggan on the back track.

The sled, Captain Anderson wrote, "was of very simple construction, being an oak board 14 inches wide, ten feet long, split with the grain and curved at the front end so as to glide through the snow easily." It carried a load of two hundred pounds, consisting of the blankets of the party, a buffalo robe each, four days' provisions, frozen fish for the dogs, an ax, a frying pan and a teapot. All this was wrapped in two green buffalo hides and lashed with rawhide. "With the exception of the surly old dog 'Major' whose place was nearest the sled, the leader 'Caribou' and the middle dog 'Moreau' cheerfully came up when they were called, put their heads in their collars and made no objection to going into harness." As they were about to start Anderson noticed a large brown dog "standing like a gentleman at the camp fire, looking on at these proceedings, possibly congratulating himself that he had not to work for his living. I enquired whose dog he was, and was told that he had followed the depot party from Pembina, that he belonged to no one in particular and that they called him 'Rover.' " At that one of the voyageurs suggested resting Moreau, a young dog, for a day so Rover was harnessed in his place. Rover seemed startled at first but pulled willingly enough between the other dogs until the day's end.

With one voyageur out in front breaking trail through the drifts, another cracking a whip and shouting *"marche"* to the dogs and Captain Anderson bringing up the rear,

the party moved off across frozen Lake Roseau. Beyond
this they traveled up a stream bed and through iced-over
swamps for five or six hours, until striking a snowshoe
track from the opposite direction. This led them after a
time to a boundary cutting, which in turn brought them,
staggering with weariness, into the surveyors' camp long
past dark. They had covered twenty-seven miles in twelve
hours, and were now within a dozen miles of the Lake of
the Woods.

Captain Anderson started back for Pine River depot
within twelve hours, only to be caught in a three-day bliz-
zard. The wind-driven snow stung and blinded the men
and dogs so that they could not face it. A temporary place
of refuge was found in a small grove of poplars, and biv-
ouac made in the lee of the roots of a blown-down tree
where a fire could be started. After an uncomfortable
night in the open, with the snow drifting over their bedding for lack of a tent, the party shifted course southward
away from the teeth of the wind. An Indian village on
Lake Roseau provided the next shelter and a much
needed night's rest. On the third day, although the storm
still raged, Anderson found it possible to cross the lake
and gain the depot. Two men from headquarters, caught
out in the same storm while hauling supplies, let their
team of horses go and for two days and nights lay in the
bottom of the sledge wrapped in buffalo robes. The
horses, finding their way back to the point of departure,
gave the alarm and brought eventual rescue.

For his third and fourth sorties from Dufferin, in February and March, Captain Anderson used dog teams entirely. During the winter most of the horses at headquarters caught the "epizootic," a kind of influenza, and
consequently could not be worked. Ox-teams were hired

locally to draw the sledges, but they were slow. In January, Lieutenant Galwey checked over the line surveyed earlier by Lieutenant Greene, east from Red River, and reported an error in it. A note in Anderson's diary read: "The result of [Galwey's] work was that the U.S. tangent runs 50′ too far south." Although the mistake favored the British, it was relayed by telegraph to the American Commissioner, and his approval of corrections asked before any final cutting out began.

Meanwhile Lieutenant Galwey was sent, early in February, to clear and mark that part of the parallel between the Lake of the Woods and Pine River, Captain Featherstonhaugh being occupied with surveying the part nearer Dufferin, toward which he was slowly progressing. In characteristic vein Galwey referred to his section, which although shorter had more timber, as "Benjamin's portion." The midwinter journey of his men to the Lake of the Woods reminded him of Saint Paul's shipwreck on Miletus: "Some getting to shore on casks, others on pieces of timber, and others any way at all (as they say in Ireland)."

During the winter Captain Cameron remained at Dufferin, except for a couple of visits to Fort Garry and an abortive trip eastward along the parallel, until the cold drove him back. In December he invited Mr. and Mrs. Herchmer to share his newly built house and provide company for Mrs. Cameron. In her honor the place was called "Emmadale." The commissary found the Commissioner "very strict on most subjects," although quite affable and kind in social relations. "When he is better used to the business and the country," wrote Herchmer, "he will better understand the almost Herculean labor required to get any satisfactory work out of the natives of this region."

In mid-January a general staff exodus to Fort Garry for a ball left Anderson and Ward the only officers in the mess. The former wrote home that the Commissioner took no charge of the work, yet was prone to criticize. This vexation was considerably mollified, however, when Captain Cameron praised his chief astronomer handsomely in a report to Sir Edward Thornton, the British Minister in Washington. In February the Commissioner visited Fort Garry for several weeks on business and he was there again in March, buying horses. His second absence and that of all the other officers happened to coincide with an official visit to Dufferin by the Bishop of Rupert's Land. After a very chilly ride in the stage from Fort Garry, His Grace found no one at headquarters to greet him but Mrs. Cameron and Mrs. Herchmer.

In early March when the British parties were already concentrated in the field to finish marking the boundary eastward along the parallel, word was received from the American Commissioner that he could not accept their work as final. His telegram came in answer to the British message, sent some time before, reporting discrepancies between Lieutenant Galwey's survey and Greene's and suggesting corrections. But Colonel Farquhar, to whom Mr. Campbell referred the matter, insisted on verification of the British fix at West Roseau, which had originally been planned as an American station. While he proceeded simply from caution, it appeared as though the disagreement in the fall over the "most northwestern point" was again bearing fruit.

Mr. Campbell's resolve was undoubtedly stiffened by a

midwinter article in the *St. Paul Pioneer Press* criticizing the American Commission for lack of effort and acquiescence. Under the caption "How the American Party Came Home on its Ear," the report stated that after running only fifty miles of line the Americans had "graciously yielded," leaving the balance to be completed by the British as they saw fit. The reporter based his story on remarks attributed to Messrs. Herchmer and Boswell on a visit to St. Paul. When taxed by Mr. Campbell with the criticism, the British Commissioner called the reported remarks "impertinent" and the article "mischievous," implying that his subordinates had been misquoted.

Before departing, March 11, for Ottawa, Captain Cameron instructed his chief astronomer to recall the British parties at once, but because of their remoteness this was not altogether practicable. Captain Anderson obtained permission to keep the working groups out until the end of the month, with the result that much of the cutting out was accomplished, even though its location would have to be checked later to the satisfaction of the Americans. Completed also was the topographical survey north of the parallel. The British realized, if the Americans did not, that such work could only be done in winter when the swamps were frozen. In the event, it was fortunate that the British parties returned as soon as they did since the last arrival at Dufferin on April 4 anticipated the spring thaw by only a few days. Even so, Captain Featherstonhaugh and his men, passing the whole winter under canvas along the line, had achieved something of an endurance record.

VI

SPRING FEVER

THE RED RIVER remained frozen over all winter to a depth of three or four feet. When the ice began to melt the river rose rapidly—as much as eight inches on April 9. By the twenty-second the level was up twenty-two feet, and a hundred yards nearer the British barracks than usual. Water backing up at ice jambs in the sharp river bends caused extensive flooding along the banks. On May 12 the river had risen thirty-two feet, coming within five feet of the level of Dufferin and filling the cellar of Captain Cameron's house. Plans were made for the lady occupants to take refuge in the upper story at headquarters and for the men in barracks to camp on higher ground, but fortunately the crest passed before this became necessary.

The flood and the "epizootic" delayed the stages from the south so no mail reached Pembina for nearly a month. Captain Cameron, returning from Ottawa late in April, was trapped at Moorhead. Meanwhile, the men and beasts of the British Commission were resting and recruiting. Four of the Canadian officers had gone home, leaving eight occupants in the headquarters building. Writing reports took up daytime hours while "a rubber of whist in the evening," wrote Captain Anderson, tided over "the hour or two after dinner when one is apt to go to sleep. We brought with us from England a capital field library, which is a great boon to the whole party." Sled dogs enjoyed an unaccustomed freedom. Ponies grazed the short new grass as soon as it appeared, and horses and oxen began to look sleek, while their drivers took to embellishing the harness with bits of colored ribbon. Three-horse teams were put to plowing a hundred acres of prairie along the river bank, soon to be enclosed with post and rails for the cultivation of vegetables and oats. This farming venture would, however, be doomed by grasshoppers in the summer.

The first steamboat, the *Selkirk*, arrived from Moorhead, May 2, with Captain Cameron and a group of Fort Garry notables on board. They tarried four or five hours at Dufferin and, according to Captain Anderson, consumed "a dozen of champagne and all that our larder and cellar could produce at the time." Soon three sternwheelers were operating on the river and passing every two or three days. A flatboat from the States also came by, loaded with potatoes, apples, butter, maple sugar, ham and eggs. Purchases were eagerly made by the inhabitants of Dufferin to relieve the diet of salt pork to which the British party had reverted when their local butcher tried to raise the price of beef. No one had cared for this dire expedient so, noted Anderson, "we all go out in the afternoon for an hour or so before dinner to a little lake on the prairie

about a mile and a half from the quarters, and by surrounding the lake we generally bring in three or four
brace of wild duck." Geese also passed overhead in large
flocks from the south but only one was shot.

The resumption of steamboat traffic coincided with a
strike of the farm laborers and axmen for more pay. But
Captain Cameron would make no concessions, and went
down to Fort Garry, on the same boat with the fifteen
men who quit, to find replacements. His wife, no doubt
bored by her long winter sojourn in Dufferin, would not
be left behind. Taking her baby along, she found the
whooping cough rampant at Fort Garry. The British
Commissioner returned in two days with twenty-eight
new men, engaged at the original wage scale of £6 a
month and everything found. The Commissioner also
recruited a troop of thirty Métis scouts, soon to be styled
the 49th Rangers. Mounted on ponies and armed with
Spencer carbines, they were intended to act as guides,
hunters and herdsmen for the advance parties reconnoitering the line westward.

These men were selected by William Hallett, a vener-
able mixed-blood hunter, who would command them. In
1869 he had scouted for Lieutenant Governor McDougall
at the time Captain Cameron was McDougall's aide-de-
camp. Of British-Indian descent and the son of a Hudson's
Bay Company factor, Hallett did not take the part of
Louis Riel in the Red River uprising, being in fact im-
prisoned by the latter's supporters on a charge of viola-
tion of parole. For deputy commander of the scouts Hallett chose a man called McDonald, and as subleaders,
three whose names were Gosselin, Lafournais and Gaddy.
As their names and visages indicated, the 49th Ranger
recruits were some of French and some of Scotch blood.

Captain Cameron was so impressed by the loyalty and character of his head scout that his final report mentioned Hallett in extravagant language: "I accompanied him on his first visit to the house of his quondam gaolers, and nothing could have been grander than the power with which his proffered hand and conciliating eye turned the distrust of his enemies into instant and concerned friendship."

The spring of 1873 saw several other additions to the staff of the British Commission. George G. Crompton, a former Royal Navy sublieutenant whose brother had been at Woolwich with Captain Anderson, applied for a job. He was made an assistant to surveyor, as was D'Arcy East, a former officer in the Royal Artillery. Both were to prove their worth later, though in a different capacity. From England came another Royal Engineers officer, Lieut. Valentine Francis Rowe. The Foreign Office had requested a special survey of the Lake of the Woods, with a view toward possibly proposing boundary changes there. This required the organization of another survey party, and afforded Captain Anderson a good reason to ask for an extra officer.

Lieutenant Rowe, of the same age and time as Galwey at Woolwich, had stood first in his class and won the Sword of Honor. He was known to the other officers of the Commission through having served at Halifax from 1867 to 1872. Captain Anderson mentioned his name and another officer's in a note to the Adjutant General, and Rowe was sent out in July with three replacements for the Royal Engineers enlisted contingent. One sapper had deserted to the States and two were invalided by rheumatism. In obtaining this extra appointment of an officer, Anderson wrote that there had been great difficulty in circumventing the Canadian Government, "as they consider they have a right to the patronage of the whole Commission."

The chief astronomer made his criticism of such a viewpoint on the grounds that the political appointments made at Ottawa disregarded any qualifications or capacity to do the work. His indignation was evidently personal, stemming from the example cited: "They appointed a man from Ottawa (who is said to be a very good groom) to be our mess cook. This worthy, after having been permitted with great forbearance to experiment with our digestions for some months, is still a very indifferent cook. We have not yet got rid of him for fear of falling into a worse trouble."

One young man joining the British Commission with qualifications quite unassailable was Dr. Thomas Millman, the assistant surgeon. He was chosen from several applicants in the graduating class in medicine at Trinity University, Toronto. It is due to his journal that many particulars of day-to-day happenings on the survey are known. Dr. Millman reached Dufferin in March, 1873, coming from eastern Canada by rail via Detroit, Chicago, St. Paul and Moorhead. From the last place he proceeded by sleigh stage 160 miles in three days, spending nights on the way at Georgetown and Grand Forks. On arrival, after calling on Dr. Burgess, he dined with the officers of the Commission and was lodged with other civilian assistants.

Dr. Millman's first task was to prepare medical supplies for the field—some sixty panniers of them—but it was not long before he found himself holding an inquest. This concerned one of the axmen in Lieutenant Galwey's party who had been struck on the head by a falling tree and killed. His body was brought into headquarters by dogsled for burial at Fort Garry. When subastronomer Coster, who had cut down the tree, gave warning of its fall, the victim had stood behind another tree for a closer look. The verdict was accidental death from a fractured skull. While still at Dufferin, Dr. Millman helped set a teamster's broken shoulder and on the same day treated an accidental gunshot wound. "Sapper McCammon went to fire off an old flintlock gun when it burst and a piece struck him in the left eye, injuring it badly." The sapper recovered from a fractured skull but lost the use of his eye. A year later he shot himself again, this time in the leg.

The great excitement at British headquarters during the spring was an Indian scare, based on misapprehensions about the Sioux. In the original estimate of costs prepared by Colonel Hawkins in 1871, the likelihood of Indian interference with the survey received attention, the conclusion being that the American parties were more apt to suffer raids than the British. Yet the possibility lingered in the mind of Her Majesty's Commissioner, and he based his recommendation for recruiting the 49th Rangers, at a cost of £4,000 a year, upon it. Captain Cameron wrote that "half-breeds afford the only means of communicating friendly intentions to the various tribes of Indians" and that they would secure scattered working parties from surprise. He also forwarded to London current reports that the Sioux would resist construction of the Northern Pacific Railway west of the Missouri River. In response to a request for instructions, should the American Commission meet with resistance, Cameron was directed by the Foreign Office to suspend operations upon arrival "in that part of the country where serious danger of attack by Indians may be apprehended."

Early in May, before these categorical instructions were received or the 49th Rangers organized, Veterinary Boswell started for Dufferin with two dozen span of Minnesota oxen and 150 horses and ponies purchased for the Commission in Ontario. Detraining at Moorhead he encountered difficulties with a crowd of supposed Fenians, who knocked him down and seized a horse, which was, however, recovered by legal process. The rise in the Red River necessitated a detour westward into Dakota Territory in order to drive the animals around the floods, and while Boswell was so occupied, a report reached Dufferin that the Sioux were concentrating. Without knowledge as to where this might occur, Captain Cameron concluded that his animals were in danger of being run off, and at once ordered out an armed party of twenty men under Captain Featherstonhaugh and Lieutenant Ward to meet Boswell. Dr. Burgess went along as medical officer. The expedition started with great spirit on the morning of May 15, but by that night a telegram arrived at headquarters reporting the horses and oxen only eighty miles away and hence out of harm's way. Cameron thereupon dispatched a Métis horseman to recall the relief force, which was overtaken after it had marched a day and a half.

Captain Anderson had nothing but praise for this abortive sortie, writing that "this little excitement has done the whole of our little community good, as we were able to show our appreciation of the well-conducted men by selecting them for this special service." Yet when Boswell's party approached the boundary real trouble arose.

The horse wranglers balked at crossing the Pembina River in flood. While still in American territory they got the worse for liquor and kicked up a great row. When they began to shoot off their revolvers and smash equipment, the soldiers at Fort Pembina were called upon to restrain them. Once again Capt. Loyd Wheaton came on the scene to pull British chestnuts out of the fire.

As the British Commission grew in engineering strength, its American counterpart diminished. Although a new appropriation in the sum of $125,000 passed Congress during the winter, without restrictions as to the hiring of technical assistance, Colonel Farquhar asked to be relieved of his post, preferring to pursue more routine engineering duties. This brought to the post of chief astronomer Maj. William Johnson Twining, who was very well qualified.

Twining was born in 1839 at Madison, Indiana, the son of a New England clergyman. Rev. William Twining, on moving west in 1836, conducted a school for girls and then became professor of mathematics, natural philosophy and astronomy at Wabash College. Young Twining's mother, from whom he derived his middle name, was a fifth generation member of the Livingston family in New York. The boy from Indiana attended Yale College briefly in 1858. The following year he received an appointment to West Point, graduating fourth in a class of twenty-five in 1863. This standing entitled him to enter the Engineer Corps, where he saw two years of active service in the Civil War, first as an assistant engineer in the Department of the Cumberland, and late in 1864, when brevetted captain, as chief engineer of the Army of the Ohio under General Schofield. In these posts he witnessed the battles of Chickamauga, Chattanooga, Atlanta and Nashville and took part in the Union march through the Carolinas. After the war, which brought him a second brevet to major, Twining spent a year teaching military engineering at West Point and in 1867, was appointed chief engineer of the Department of Dakota.

In this post, whose range encompassed all of the northwestern United States from Minnesota to Montana, Major Twining became familiar with much of the terrain that he would cover later in the boundary survey. In the summer of 1869, he made an extensive reconnaissance in northern Dakota Territory, between the Red and the Souris Rivers. Starting from Fort Abercrombie, July 14, he crossed a series of streams to arrive at Fort Totten on Devil's Lake, thence visiting Pembina Mountain and River and the lower Red River Valley, even spending a day at Fort Garry. Returning to Fort Totten by a more westward route, Twining again set out, September 1, with an escort of thirty men of the 20th Infantry, to explore the Souris River along the eastern part of its great loop into United States territory. Next he reconnoitered Turtle Mountain, a refuge of the hostile remnant of the Sisseton and Santee Sioux. On the northern slope, across the 49th parallel, he found twenty lodges, the inhabitants of which fled on his approach. Twining prepared a map of these explorations and the trails followed, which came in handy four years later.

To be sure the American major was not the first surveyor to visit the Souris River. Sixteen years before his reconnaissance, when a railroad route from the Mississippi to the Pacific coast was under exploration, Governor Isaac Stevens of Washington Territory passed that way. His report on a northern route near the 47th and 49th parallels described the Souris, and his engineer, A.W.

Tinkham, calculated the latitude of its great bend. The proposed line of track was located to head the coulées running down to the river on its western side, while its wooded valley was counted as a source for railroad ties and building stone. Later in 1853, and farther west, Tinkham reconnoitered the Milk River valley and the Sweet Grass Hills, which the boundary surveyors would also reach, to report on the availability there of lumber and ballast.

Governor Stevens' report, published in 1855, was undoubtedly available to Major Twining, and to the boundary Commissioners as background intelligence. But of all the engineer officers, British or American, assembling at Pembina in 1873, the new American chief astronomer was the only one personally familiar with the path that lay immediately westward.

VII

SUMMER ON THE PARALLEL

THE VAN of the American Commission, headed by its new chief astronomer Twining, Captain Gregory and Lieutenant Greene, reached Pembina by the steamboat *Selkirk,* June 1, but not until three weeks later did the transport train and cavalry escort arrive overland from Fort Abercrombie. For the 1873 season the American escort was composed of Captain Harbach's company of the 20th Infantry and two companies of the 7th Cavalry, Capt. Thomas B. Weir commanding Company D and Capt. Myles W. Keogh, Company I. Maj. Marcus A. Reno, 7th Cavalry, had the overall command. The engineer officers left Fort Pembina, June 9, with two astronomical parties under Twining and Gregory and a tangent survey party under Greene.

Descended from a brother of Gen. Nathanael Greene, Francis Vinton Greene was born in 1850 at Providence,

Rhode Island. His father, Brevet Maj. Gen. George Sears Greene, was a West Pointer, class of 1823, and a civil engineer. It was the brigade commanded by him that held Culp's Hill against the Confederate assault on the second day of the battle of Gettysburg. Young Greene graduated from West Point in 1870 at the head of his class. Commissioned a second lieutenant in the 4th Artillery, he transferred to the Corps of Engineers in 1872, and the boundary survey was his initial engineering assignment. Greene was five years junior to Captain Gregory, who graduated from West Point in 1865 and for several years had been assigned to the geodetic survey of the Great Lakes. He was the son of the Rev. Oscar H. Gregory, minister of the Dutch Reformed Church in Troy, New York. Neither Twining, Gregory nor Greene were married.

A new recruit to the American Commission was Dr. Elliott Coues, assistant surgeon in the army and a distinguished ornithologist. He held the appointment of medical officer and naturalist in the Commission, and arrived with Archibald Campbell at Fort Pembina about the middle of June. His medical duties were not arduous, if a note addressed to the American Commissioner can be taken as typical. Reporting on the "result of repeated trials of the use of 'Persian Insect Powders' as a defense against mosquitoes," Dr. Coues wrote, "the article is a perfect failure." James E. Bangs, secretary of the Commission, made a third member of Mr. Campbell's entourage.

Meanwhile the British Commission had already taken the field. Commissioner Cameron issued operating instructions in forty-six paragraphs, dividing his party into seven departments, with separately defined duties. Topographical, Commissariat, Medical, Veterinary, Natural

History, Intelligence and Headquarters, each had its own head reporting to the Commissioner, but the chief astronomer, given charge of the Topographical Department, was also authorized to issue orders to any member of the British contingent. The rationale of this elaborate directive may be found in a paragraph stating that previously "a large responsibility" had been thrown upon the leaders of parties and "greater freedom of action" allowed them than "it is considered to be in the interest of the service to continue." Perhaps the Commissioner realized that he had been taking a back seat. Yet he could still do so under a further instruction that "while thus limiting the authority of heads of departments and members . . . any responsibility they may incur which is plainly to the advantage of the service yet incompatible with previous reference for authority will not only be approved of but expected of them as a matter of duty."

The instructions ended in a paragraph dealing with Indians, whose susceptibilities the Commissioner, following the dictates of the Foreign Office, was most anxious not to offend. For three hundred miles west of Pembina a friendly reception of the surveyors seemed likely, but all members of the Commission were strictly enjoined to show the Indians "every consideration" and to avoid "even the appearance of contempt toward them." Powwows should be avoided by referral to the Commissioner and by explaining the Queen's object of simply marking a line with the Americans, beyond which the latter would not encroach. The formula for conciliation ended: "Nothing could cause Her Majesty greater dissatisfaction than that any of her servants should cause Her friends the Indians to doubt the kindly feeling for them, or to forget that they have always been at peace with Her." If Commissioner Cameron contemplated giving out food or presents, he said nothing about it.

On May 12, the first party of surveyors left Dufferin, in charge of Sergeant Kay, R.E., to commence mapping a six-mile belt north of the parallel from Red River. He was to cover the territory westward to Pembina River, where Mr. Russell had the next sector. Beyond Russell came Colonel Forrest. Lieutenant Galwey took out the first astronomical party May 26th, to a station 20 miles west on the line known as Point Michel, while Captain Featherstonhaugh left, June 7, for a position on the east side of Pembina Mountain, 35 miles out. These particular astronomical stations were observed by both Commissions, and with the respective results differing by only ten and twenty-nine feet, the chief astronomers agreed to carry on observations at alternate stations.

In mid-June Major Twining made the fix for the United States at Point Michel and Captain Gregory at East Pembina. To keep the American parties together until their transport and cavalry escort arrived, the next station at West Pembina, 47 miles from Red River, was observed by Lewis Boss, a civilian assistant in Major Twining's party, with Captain Gregory following at Long River, 77 miles west. In the interim Lieutenant Galwey and Captain Featherstonhaugh passed beyond the American astronomers, to fix positions at Sleepy Hollow, 95 miles from Red River, and on the east side of Turtle Mountain, 115 miles out, which they respectively reached around the beginning of July. With the arrival of Major Reno and his cavalry at the last point, the plan to rotate observations between the Commissions could be implemented to alternate every other station instead of every other two.

Meanwhile Captain Anderson, finding that the American Commission would have but two astronomical parties in the field, devoted himself to advance reconnaissance. With twenty mounted men of the 49th Rangers he left Dufferin, June 11, for a trip along the parallel, to locate a route and camping places for those to follow. Beyond Pembina Mountain, a wooded elevation three hundred feet above the prairie, he crossed an old track used by traders from Red River, following it for several days until it turned southwest. Taking a new course across the prairie he explored westerly as far as Turtle Mountain, another wooded elevation of several hundred feet, choosing en route second stations for Galwey and Featherstonhaugh when they had finished farther east. After selecting a site for a principal supply depot 120 miles from Red River, the British chief astronomer left Turtle Mountain. He reached Dufferin on June 23, his return coinciding with the arrival at Pembina of the American transport and cavalry. Captain Anderson wrote home, "We saw no Indians tho' our scouts tried very hard to find some." Yet he encountered enemies far more implacable. "We were terribly tortured by mosquitoes, which were in myriads along our track and gave us no rest. It was impossible to keep them out of our food and at night neither men nor animals got any rest . . . The horses suffer terribly, and we are obliged to tie them up at night to prevent them running away beyond reach of capture."

Lieutenant Galwey reported his experiences in similar vein. To see Pembina Mountain rising from the prairie "was like sighting land after being at sea for a month . . . As for mosquitoes their very name makes me shudder." If all the plagues of Egypt were amalgamated into one it would not have been a patch on them. He found the daytime heat excessive, on an average 90 degrees, but took consolation in cool nights, with the temperature down to 36 degrees. "It is an awful country for thunderstorms. We have had no less than thirteen bad ones since the 4th of the month. They are always accompanied with a violent gale and rain. I had to rush out of my tent with nothing on but my night shirt, could not even wait to find my boots, to save my tent from being swept away. I found it held by only two guys and did not the mosquitoes take an unfair advantage. They completely outflanked me."

From his next station the Anglo-Irish lieutenant wrote, "I christened the point Sleepy Hollow as all the men slept I think for at least eighteen hours on the stretch." This was after an advance of eighty miles in three days. He had experienced another thunderstorm and with his night-shirt blowing over his head felt like "an old woman struggling with an umbrella turned inside out." The sappers were highly amused but Galwey had the last laugh: "I have found out a very good way of making my tent stand up, *viz.*, by turning out all my men whenever it blows down. It is wonderful the care they bestow in pitching it now." On July 18, Galwey was camped with Captain Featherstonhaugh at Turtle Mountain depot when Commissioner Campbell arrived from Pembina to confer with Major Twining and the other American officers. Galwey noted "the place presents the appearance of a town, two of the American parties being camped here with an escort of 70 infantry and 160 cavalry. So all lodge together. There must be 500 men here."

Captain Anderson missed this concentration, as he was off on a second reconnaissance a hundred miles farther to the west. This time he took with him twenty-five mounted scouts and two light wagons. Observations with

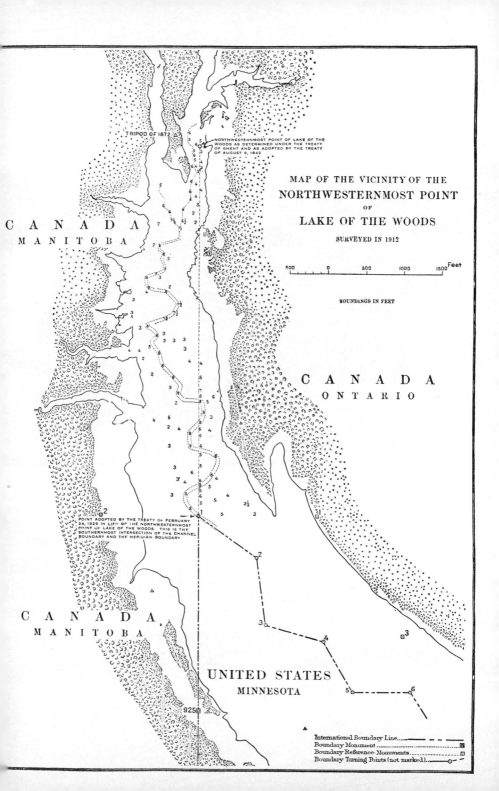

TRIPOD OF 1872 △

NORTHWESTEHNMOST POINT OF LAKE OF THE
WOODS AS DETERMINED UNDER THE TREATY
OF GHENT AND AS ADOPTED BY THE TREATY
OF AUGUST 9, 1842

MAP OF THE VICINITY OF THE
NORTHWESTERNMOST POINT
OF
LAKE OF THE WOODS
SURVEYED IN 1912

500   0   500   1000   1500 Feet

SOUNDINGS IN FEET

C A N A D A
MANITOBA

C A N A D A
ONTARIO

POINT ADOPTED BY THE TREATY OF FEBRUARY
24, 1925 IN LIEU OF THE NORTHWESTERNMOST
POINT OF LAKE OF THE WOODS. THIS IS THE
SOUTHERNMOST INTERSECTION OF THE CHANNEL
BOUNDARY AND THE MERIDIAN BOUNDARY

C A N A D A
MANITOBA

UNITED STATES
MINNESOTA

925

International Boundary Line............
Boundary Monument.............................
Boundary Reference Monuments...........
Boundary Turning Points (not marked)....

Royal Engineers "Relief Force"; Dr. Burgess, Capt. Featherstonhaugh, Capt. Ward FRONT ROW L. TO R.

Steamer *Dakota* at Dufferin UPPER LEFT
Pub. Archives Canada

Dakota at Upper Fort Garry LOWER LEFT
Int. Boundary Comm.

Ox Trains on the Boundary Trail RIGHT

Observatory Tent and Zenith Telescope BELOW
Int. Boundary Comm.

Turtle Mountain Cutting, sketched by Alfred Downing
New York Public Library

La Roche Percée UPPER LEFT
Int. Boundary Comm.

Pembina Mountain Depot LOWER LEFT
Millman

Sep 24th/73 —
Pyramid creek

Sketch by Lieut. Rowe

Pub. Archives Canada

The Same Scene Photographed

Millman

a sextant would establish latitude within a hundred yards while pocket chronometers afforded a sufficient measurement of distance. British astronomical stations were sited at the first and second crossings of the Souris River (170 and 215 miles from Red River) and another main depot located at the farther point. At its first crossing, the Souris or Mouse River flowed north through a low marshy valley about a mile wide and fifty feet below the prairie. The stream, deep and nearly stagnant, was ninety feet wide. At the second crossing the river ran south in a 200-foot deep valley, a mile and a half across. Here the flow was rapid and clear over a gravelly bottom, easily fordable. Lieutenant Galwey would advance to observe at both these locations, while Major Twining and Captain Gregory occupied intermediate stations at West Turtle Mountain (150 miles) and South Antler Creek (193 miles). The British chief astronomer returned to Turtle Mountain in time to give the Americans, who had remained in camp, the benefit of the information collected by him on routes, fords, wood and water. Anderson wrote home that "Captain Cameron appeared like a comet the night I returned, and after talking to me for two hours while I lay in bed very tired, went off to Pembina at six the next morning."

This hasty call resulted from the fact that when the two Commissioners had met in Pembina at the beginning of July, another disagreement between them arose. Captain Cameron, apparently ignoring the advice of his chief astronomer, proposed that the boundary be marked as a mean parallel, that is to say, by averaging the local variations of all the astronomical points fixed along it, so as to achieve a more perfect curve. Major Twining objected to the cost of such a procedure, since it meant relocating each fix after the whole had been completed. But the British Commissioner insisted that such a curve was what the term "parallel" in the treaty required. In a letter to Mr. Campbell the next day he deprecated the alternative as "the patchy parallel which would result from ignoring self-evident errors in the location of individual points determined astronomically only." Since this was exactly what both astronomers had been doing since the beginning, Commissioner Campbell would not let the criticism pass unchallenged. For good measure he declined to sign the minutes of their meetings, which his opposite number had prepared.

This refusal further embarrassed Captain Cameron, who had introduced into the minutes a reference to the "loop" at the Northwest Angle where the due south line crossed the meandering channel line of the northwest arm, stating that the American chief astronomer had called attention to it. He was, of course, laying the ground for future reconsideration of the "anomalous intersection" as he had previously suggested to the Foreign Office. But Mr. Campbell smelled a rat in the mention of his own astronomer and wished the entire reference omitted. He also declined to concur in a report or map on the position of the "most northwestern point" while Captain Cameron persisted in not accepting the site of the reference monument as pointed out by the Indians. This frustrated the British Commissioner's effort to comply with instructions from the Foreign Office to avoid discussion and submit a joint report. These differences between the Commissioners remained outstanding for the rest of 1873, although their chief astronomers continued to co-operate.

On September 11, the Commissioners met again at

Wood End depot. As noted in the diary of Secretary Bangs: "Captain Cameron calls in the morning and has an interview with Mr. Campbell—lively time. Plain talk —invite him and Ward to dinner. He comes but not Ward. Very pleasant time—duck, beef, all the luxuries of the season. He stays till 9—*buzzing* Com'r." The tenor of the conversation may be inferred from a letter written by the British Commissioner two days later. He protested vehemently that his expression "patchy" had not been used disrespectfully nor had it been intended to imply contempt for Campbell's opinion. On the same date, Bangs's diary recorded: "Twining and Reno call on British Commissioner. Came back *full* of *spirits*." It would seem that they at least had been conciliated. But a few days later, after receiving from Captain Ward a bill of $7,141.65 for clearing the line east of Red River, Campbell was still unhappy. Bangs noted: "Mr. C. expatiates on the enormity of Cameron's bill for cutting. He may kick, but of course we'll have to take their word for it." Still later: "Commissioner takes the day to 'interview' me (the Dr. being out shooting). Long conversation in which Cameron, Farquhar, Twining, Coues and everybody generally gets a good scoring."

To fortify his position on the northwest point, the American Commissioner asked Major Twining for an opinion as to whether the objection of Captain Cameron to the Indians' site was tenable. Most diplomatically, in case the letter be shown to the British, Twining wrote that in his view the British Commissioner might, "without being considered as acting in an obstructive manner," take the ground that the evidence was not conclusive; but in making such objection, it was incumbent on him to suggest some other point as the "most northwestern" which the shape of the bay would render possible. This, of course, Captain Cameron never did, and probably could not have done to British advantage.

VIII

FOUR HUNDRED MILES WEST

WHILE the British astronomers were on station taking observations of the stars, it was the task of their assistants to survey a tangent line toward the next station so as to connect with it. The tangent was laid off at right angles to the meridian of the first station, and continued in a straight line by chain and transit until it struck the meridian of the second. Then right angle offsets from the tangent to the parallel were computed and measured on the ground at intervals from one to three miles where permanent marks on the parallel would be erected. To the western boundary of Manitoba (then 181 miles from Red River) the interval adopted was a mile; farther west it averaged three. Captain Featherstonhaugh calculated that the time occupied in determining the latitude at each station averaged a week, three clear nights being sufficient for observations. For the final fix a zenith telescope was employed in observing north and south stars. On the prairie the work of surveying the tangent, or running the line, as it was called, progressed at about five miles a day, there being no timber to cut through. The intervals between astronomical stations varied from twelve to thirty-five miles, the longest being across Turtle Mountain.

Here, as at Pembina Mountain, there was wooded terrain consisting of numerous small hills covered with poplar, birch and oak. Between them were many swamps and lakes, since the water was unable to drain off. Captain Featherstonhaugh's party started cutting out the tangent line from the east side of Turtle Mountain on July 15. On the west side an American party under Lieutenant Greene began cutting also, moving eastward. They accomplished ten miles to a mile-long lake, subsequently named for Colonel Farquhar; then Greene, who had charge of running all the tangents for the American Commission, had to move on. Captain Featherstonhaugh soon left the task of continuing the cutting to Messrs. King and Ashe, his assistant astronomers. With great persistence the British party finished twenty-four miles to join up with the American sector late in September. Of the density of the trees, Lieutenant Greene wrote to his parents from the Turtle Mountain cutting: "To pitch a camp it was necessary to cut away an undergrowth of poplars so thick that I could hear but not see a motion of a man cutting at twenty feet from me."

On July 31, Captain Anderson left Turtle Mountain depot for his third reconnaissance, accompanied by Commissary Herchmer. Beyond the second crossing of the Souris River they followed an old traders' road much of the way, passing Rivière des Lacs (237 miles west of Red River), where Major Twining would soon observe, and

Short Creek, Captain Featherstonhaugh's next station (255 miles west). Five miles past this point they came to a creek beyond which trees did not grow, and christened this depot site "Wood End." Here Captain Anderson left a garrison of thirty men to cut and stack firewood for his parties going beyond. Apprehension that the Americans "with their little army of cavalry and infantry" would also camp at this point and make short work of the wood supply did not materialize. The third reconnaissance was extended as far as the Great Coteau, a rough escarpment rising abruptly from the prairie and cutting obliquely across the parallel in a northwesterly direction at 289 miles west of Red River. Here an astronomical station was sited for Lieutenant Galwey and a subdepot located later.

On the second day of this journey the party met its first encampment of Sioux, who were friendly enough to allow themselves to be photographed. The scouts saw a few antelope and shot one. An old buffalo bull scampered away from them across the plains. On the traders' road Captain Anderson met a Métis who "had a caravan of carts loaded with dried meat for sale at Fort Garry, and in front of the caravan in a spring wagon were his wife and family, all of a very dusky hue." These people came from Woody Mountain, a settlement of Métis hunters near the buffalo country.

Dr. Millman, who visited the Turtle Mountain depot in July, wrote, "it consists of a large long building, and a shed beside it contains the harness and smith shop and the carpenter's shop." He joined Lieutenant Galwey's party at the second Souris crossing, where his ambulance was accidentally toppled into the water. "On the east bank were camped the American cavalry. The Stars and Stripes waving on one side of the river and the Union

Jack on the other, presented the appearance of two enemies encamped." But it was the sight of Sioux tepees that led him to procure from the depot "a Spencer rifle for myself and two for my teamster, with fifteen rounds of cartridges for each." For small game the young doctor had been lent a shotgun by the Commissioner. Returning toward Turtle Mountain in September, Dr. Millman observed a band of fifty Indians crossing the prairie. He noted in his diary: "They intend to remain in the mountains all winter to hunt . . . One or two of them could speak English fluently. These Indians had a hand in the Minnesota Massacre, 1862. I believe they have two or three white girls with them whom they captured at that time." A later entry reflected Captain Cameron's instructions: "The Indians had a pow-wow with the Commissioner. They were jubilant on seeing him. Expecting a liberal present from him, they all shook hands. He ordered depot-man Ellis to give each of them two plugs of tobacco, two pounds of flour and three of beans."

The American Commission moved its main base from Turtle Mountain to the second Souris crossing, about a hundred miles farther west, at the end of July. While Company K of the 20th Infantry continued to supply escorts for working parties, Company I of the 7th Cavalry accompanied the supply train and cattle herd to the new base. Major Reno, with Company D, set out for Fort Stevenson, Dakota Territory, to bring up another supply train. This was met at the great bend of the Souris River. As a compliment to the departmental commander, the new base received the name of Camp Terry.

In his report at the end of the season Major Reno took exception "to the uses made by the small parties of the mounted men who were furnished as guard . . . They were used virtually as assistants by the parties for which they were escorts. This was particularly so with the topographical parties, when, in addition to the generally regular march of twenty miles, they would be sent a distance of five miles south of the line, and be used as flag bearers, to station themselves as sight at the head of ravines, etc., consuming that time that care and attention to grazing renders necessary, when the allowance of forage is reduced." With no Indians to fight, Major Reno had little inclination to help the surveyors at the expense of his horses. This unco-operative attitude on the part of the cavalryman manifested itself chiefly toward the civilians who led the topographical parties. Captain Gregory had only four cavalry troopers with him, and Greene none until after September 1, when a detachment under Lieut. R.H.L. Alexander escorted him beyond the Coteau.

In 1873, Lieutenant Greene organized two topographical parties respectively under Frederick Von Schrader and Alfred Downing, the former being succeeded in September by Charles L. Doolittle. They managed to complete the mapping of a six-mile belt of territory south of the parallel to a point 385 miles west of Red River. The British, with three parties, covered 400 miles north of the line, in a belt from six to fifteen miles wide. The greater part was accomplished by two Royal Engineers, Sergeant Kay and Corporal Malings, the latter taking over the leadership of Mr. Russell's party on August 1st when the civilian surveyor resigned his appointment. All the topographers paid particular attention to watercourses and the valleys in which they flowed.

Two remarkable features found in the British topographical belt between the second and third crossings of the Souris River were the Hill of the Murdered Scout and La Roche Percée. The former, an isolated butte over-looking the valley of the Souris to the north and the Rivière des Lacs to the southeast, derived its name from a legendary Assiniboine deed in 1830. One member of a war party of these Indians, climbing the hill to watch the surrounding country, came upon an enemy rolled up in a buffalo robe fast asleep. Seizing a rock, the Assiniboine bashed in the head of the sleeper and, to commemorate the deed, scooped out in the gravelly soil the figure of a man lying at full length with legs and arms outstretched. Major Twining, who credited this tale, wrote that the marks, though only a few inches deep, were still distinctly visible when he visited the spot. "In the hollow represent-ing the head of the murdered man there was a red granite stone, smooth, oblong in shape, and about eight inches in greatest diameter, which was said to have been the stone used."

In the Souris Valley, a few miles to the west of the Hill of the Murdered Scout, the surveyors came upon a series of eroded rocks of soft sandstone underlying a capping of harder stone; some were pierced through so as to give the appearance of ruined dwellings with window openings. Captain Anderson noted that the soft rock bore in many places "rude Indian carvings with birds and other ani-mals." In one of the photographs taken by the Royal En-gineers of La Roche Percée, there also appeared cut in the stone the legend: "J. M. & G. P. Photographers B. N. A. B. C. S. Sept. 10, 1873." This, strangely enough, is the only clue remaining today of the identity of the sappers who served as photographers for the British Commission. The initial carvers were named McCammon and Parsons.

"Topoging" the creeks near the third crossing of the Souris, one of Lieutenant Greene's parties had the excitement of discovering coal. "It occurs in seams from one to ten feet thick and crops out through the clay in the vertical bluffs below the prairie bordering the creek," he wrote. "It is brown coal or lignite and is in the belt of the Missouri River Lignite described in all geologies. I have tried it in my forge and it works well enough for ordinary work, bending iron, etc., but will not do for welding." Dawson the geologist took an equally keen interest in these deposits, which he believed had a tendency to burn away below ground if outcroppings were ignited by prairie fires. Farther west he found one bed with a seam of lignite eighteen feet thick and measuring 46 per cent carbon.

Captain Anderson's fourth reconnaissance began when he left Wood End, September 5, to penetrate the Great Coteau. At the station previously sited there, he found Lieutenant Galwey who had just come up; still farther ahead at Mid-Coteau (312 miles west) was Captain Gregory, out in front of the British for the first time on the line. With Lieutenant Greene running tangents for him, the second American astronomer was able to take over the remainder of the United States stations, observing seven altogether during the summer. Major Twining observed three, thereafter making his base at the Wood End depot. Like Captain Anderson, he exercised general supervision over the whole commission. After Mid-Coteau Gregory would move on to Bully Spring, 363 miles west, named by his men for the excellent quality of the water. He would finish at West Poplar River, 408 miles from Red River, late in September. This stream was the first considerable watercourse flowing southeast toward the Missouri River. Captain Anderson located Galwey's last station on the eastern branch of it, called by him Porcupine Creek, 385 miles out. Here he turned back, September 13, for the dépot at Wood End.

The Great Coteau, some forty-five miles across at the 49th parallel, formed what Captain Anderson called the second steppe on the prairie west of Red River, the first being Pembina Mountain. It consisted of a bare elevation, rising abruptly two or three hundred feet above the prairie, but broken up into an irregular crisscross of ridges, valleys, cones and hollows with no distinct watershed. Beyond it the British chief astronomer came to a more undulating country, with many alkaline lakes having no outlets. His first sight of the Missouri watershed was a valley two miles wide and 250 feet deep, the stream at the bottom almost dried up. But stunted trees grew there and Anderson called the station, which he sited nearby, "Big Muddy" (338 miles west of Red River). Captain Featherstonhaugh occupied it, September 14, and Lieutenant Rowe, who had just reached the end of the line, traced the tangent west.

Early in September several of the field parties were threatened by prairie fires sweeping erratically through the dry grass. A far-off pillar of smoke to the north heralded their coming. Backfiring to save the camp or burning a patch on the prairie in which to take refuge comprised the usual methods of defense. Lieutenant Galwey, approaching the subdepot at the Great Coteau, noticed a fire in the distance, then saw smoke at the camp as its occupants started a backfire. But this got out of control, raced away, and then with a shift in the wind returned in the night. "We all had to turn out to keep the fire away from the tents," wrote Galwey, who "found everyone looking like a lot of demons from the soot and smoke." The next morning, thinking all was well, he sent out a party to build the earth mounds that marked the boundary in treeless and rockless country. "They had a very narrow shave of it as the fire came on them very suddenly. They just had time to fire the prairie in front of them and gallop the horses on to the burnt portion. One man had his hat burned up. All lost some hair and were obliged to lie down on the hot ground to escape being stifled by smoke."

Featherstonhaugh and Rowe, approaching the depot that same morning, didn't have time to burn the grass in front. Instead they galloped their horses through the flames. "Luckily," Galwey observed, "the grass at the spot was very short." Lieutenant Rowe noted that the grass was seldom higher than the knees, but when burning as high as the saddle it was a great peril. A fire also overtook a commissary wagon train drawn by spans of oxen. Although a patch of ground was burnt, and the unyoked oxen driven to it, the animals would not remain quiet but rushed about wildly as the flames came by and were badly singed in the legs.

Lieutenant Greene came upon the burnt-over prairie district with a hundred head of horses and mules in his train, as well as a small herd of beef cattle. In doubt whether to go on because of the animals, he relied on his scout's assurance that there were plenty of swamps near the Coteau where the grass was too wet to burn. "In half an hour we were entirely out of sight of grass, nothing before or behind us or on either side as far as the eye could reach but a pitch black expanse, dotted with buffalo skeletons looking whiter and more ghastly than ever." Crossing the Coteau he found only three pools of surface water where there was grass, and that unburnt only when actually growing out of water. The lack of green fodder would become a serious matter when the surveyors began their 400-mile retreat from the field.

Meanwhile another hazard had to be faced—the equinoctial storm, which struck almost the same day as the year before. Flocks of duck and geese winging south again gave brief warning. It blew, sleeted and snowed for four days and nights, immobilizing the working parties for nearly a week. Featherstonhaugh, Gregory, Galwey and Greene, on station in treeless country beyond the Coteau, took what shelter they could in ravines. Major Twining found a safe refuge in the wooded valley of the Souris at Wood End, and Captain Anderson at the Coteau sub-depot. Captain Cameron, who had driven as far as this point in a light wagon at the beginning of September, returned to Dufferin ahead of the storm.

Hardly waiting until the storm was over, Captain Anderson set out on his final reconnaissance, to explore beyond the last American station at West Poplar Creek. Traveling in snow, he reached this point on October 2 and after a day storm-bound in camp, selected a site for the first British station of the next season at 432 miles west of Red River. Here the well-wooded ravines and streams ran southwesterly in the direction of the Milk River. Twelve buffalo in two groups were seen in the vicinity. Turning back, October 7, the British chief astronomer fell in with a mounted party of Sioux who had just come from the Métis settlement at Woody Mountain. The opportunity for further exploration was too good to be missed. Following the back track of the Indians for twenty-five miles in the snow, Captain Anderson came upon the huts of the hunters in a well-wooded and sheltered valley twenty-two miles north of the boundary and 420 miles from Red River, as the crow flies. He learned that eighty families of French half-breeds, mostly migrants from St. Joseph on Pembina River, wintered there, though all but a few were off on their fall buffalo hunt. These Métis made periodic trips to Fort Peck and Fort Benton on the Missouri River, or sometimes to Fort Garry, to exchange buffalo meat and robes for flour and other supplies.

IX

RETURN TO BASE

CAPTAIN GREGORY completed his observations at West Poplar River, September 30, and was the first of the astronomers to retreat. He arrived at Wood End, October 6, his horses and mules worn out and exhausted from lack of forage. With Major Twining he returned to Camp Terry and thence the American train and escort started for Fort Totten across the burned-over plains. They arrived, October 20, shortly before Lieutenant Greene, who had pushed the topographical survey to the 385-mile point by October 3 before starting his retreat. From Fort Totten all the members of the American Commission except Greene left to board the Northern Pacific Railway at Jamestown, Dakota Territory; Greene was ordered back to Fort Pembina to resurvey the parallel between Red River and the Lake of the Woods during the winter.

During the march from the field Major Reno sprained

his ankle—so he reported in November from Harrisburg, Pennsylvania, after thirty days' sick leave. But because he forwarded no surgeon's certificate of continuing disability, the Paymaster General stopped his pay and noted him "absent without leave." On January 2, 1874, Reno was still away from his station at Fort Totten, and wrote to the Adjutant General from New York that he was about to start for Chicago to see General Sheridan and straighten things out. The letter concluded, "I only hope I can arrange matters so as not to resign." The major and the general were old comrades in arms—the former having served the latter as chief of staff for cavalry in the Shenandoah Valley in 1864. Reno's explanation of his absence was evidently accepted, but had it not been, he might have escaped a worse fate later on.

The British Commission retraced their steps about the same time as the Americans. On October 3, Captain Featherstonhaugh turned over his party to Lieutenant Rowe at Pyramid Creek and hurried back to inspect the cutting at Turtle Mountain. While tracing his last tangent to West Poplar, Lieutenant Galwey ran out of firewood; he burned the tables, stools and floor of the observatory tent instead. Returning to camp on finishing the line, he found "they had burned the doctor's stretcher to cook dinner." With enough oats to feed his horses 6 lbs. a day for four days, he was able to overtake Captain Gregory, who could only feed his mules 3 lbs. daily. But five of Galwey's horses gave out and one died before the Coteau depot, with its supply of oats, could be reached. At Wood End Galwey rested his teams a day and a half; at the second Souris crossing he "found the prairie burned but luckily during the summer they had made hay and stacked it at 25-mile intervals." Galwey reached Dufferin, October 20, having traveled 440 miles in twenty days, walking three hundred of them himself. Captain Anderson was the last to return, leaving Wood End depot with Dr. Burgess and the third surveying party on October 20. They arrived at headquarters on the last day of the month, three days after a freeze closed the Red River to navigation.

With no winter surveying to do, all the Royal Engineers officers received leaves. Only Anderson and Ward stayed on at headquarters; early in November, Featherstonhaugh, Rowe and Galwey left for eastern Canada to pass the winter in Halifax. Galwey spent three days in Chicago en route and came to the conclusion that "American ladies dress wonderfully; American men swear horribly and spit profusely." He praised the American hotels but found their charges high. "Cost me £5 for two days. For that I had excellent fare, comfortable quarters and the pleasure of seeing a Yankee eating a hardboiled egg with a knife."

At Dufferin there was much activity building storehouses and stabling for the two hundred horses and oxen of the Commission. According to Dr. Millman, cellars were dug to a depth of three feet. "They then put poles over in a gable-like manner so that there are two lengths of poles on each side. The lower poles are covered with straw and earth, the upper ones only with straw. Owing to there being no rain or thaw during the winter, they answer very well. They accommodate two rows of horses. They have six of these stables each holding over thirty horses. The farm was a complete failure."

Captain Cameron left Dufferin for Ottawa in mid-October, taking his wife with him. At her father's insistence, she was returning to the Tupper home at St.

Andrews, New Brunswick, for the winter. Sir John Macdonald's government had fallen so Dr. Tupper was no longer a Dominion cabinet minister. "We shall get on all the better for not having any back stairs influence at work," wrote Captain Anderson, adding that "Capt. C. and the American Commissioner never agree upon anything, and it is very humiliating to find one's own superior so overbearing and continually putting himself in the wrong box."

The British Commissioner returned to Dufferin early in December. He had about made up his mind (so he told Anderson) to recognize the site of the reference monument as pointed out by the Indians at the northwest point, but was as insistent as ever on a mean parallel. His readiness to concede the first issue was perhaps due to the fact that during the past summer D'Arcy East had thoroughly examined the country west of the Lake of the Woods comprising the Northwest Angle and reported it practically all swamp or muskeg. Mr. East also expressed the opinion that a road could be made around the northwest point so as to connect the lake and the Dawson Road entirely through British soil. Captain Cameron had himself visited the area in August, so was now in a position to forward to the Foreign Office the special survey it had requested, even though Mr. Campbell would not join therein. This Cameron did, February 4, 1874, repeating, however, his skepticism about the monument and referring to the "loop." To discredit the Indians' disclosure to James McKay, Cameron cited their earlier effort to extract payment for pointing out the location.

At the same time the British Commissioner asked the Foreign Office for instructions as to whether he should mark an astronomical parallel or a mean one, estimating the extra cost of the latter at £50,000. The expense, he thought, "however it may affect the public interests, does not bear upon the merits of the question," and "appears to be beyond my province to consider." His penchant for the more perfect curve had given rise to his latest disagreement with Mr. Campbell, and Captain Cameron was also at odds over it with his own chief astronomer. The point so concerned Captain Anderson that he decided to take a hand, unofficially, to influence the Foreign Office decision. Accordingly, on February 7, he wrote to his brother officer Wilson, now a major, at the War Office: "We have already run the astronomical parallel for 500 miles, built the mounds, and I have estimated that in conjunction with the Americans we can complete the demarcation of the astronomical parallel to the summit of the Rocky Mountains this season . . . To mark a mean parallel will involve another season's work over the whole ground again, and is altogether opposed to the views of Mr. Campbell and his chief astronomer, with whom I am in perfect accord. Surely the Foreign Office would never consent to this most unnecessary waste of public money, merely to move the boundary mounds a few feet north and south and still to be no nearer the truth."

Major Wilson lost no time in passing this "private" letter on to Cabinet circles, his covering note commenting: "The question of a mean parallel is no new one; it was often discussed by the members of the Oregon Boundary Commission of which I was secretary and the opinion of Colonel Hawkins, Major Haig and the other officers was opposed to it on the ground that the mere adjustment of the boundary at certain points in a country unsuitable for settlement or pasturage would certainly not justify the enormous expense of running a mean parallel."

Thus Captain Cameron's viewpoint, although endorsed by the Privy Council of the Dominion Government, met with immediate challenge at the Foreign Office. There a change of ministers had just resulted from Disraeli's victory over Gladstone in a general election. Lord Derby, replacing Lord Granville, sought expert advice on the two boundary questions awaiting his attention. He referred the matter of the monument to none other than Major Wilson, and the question of parallels to the Astronomer Royal.

The major, already well-informed through previous correspondence with Captain Anderson, simplified the first issue by pointing out that the only alternative to the Indians' site would be to fix the northwest point where the channel of the arm cut the latitude of 49° 23′ 55″ given by Dr. Tiarks. Such a location would move the due south line (already cut) 108 feet west, thus giving the United States more territory. As to the "loop" it would exist in any case and might be left for future settlement between the two governments. His common-sense view met with Lord Derby's approval, who passed it on to the British Commissioner for guidance.

The Astronomer Royal had in fact advised Captain Anderson before the Commission left England that an astronomical parallel would satisfy the treaty. When asked by Lord Derby he reiterated this opinion, feeling that the treaty contemplated "a series of points whose undisputed latitude is 49° 0′ 0″." Such points could be joined with sufficient accuracy by straight lines, although a little would be gained in accuracy by lines of lateral curvature, as on the surface of the sea. The discrepancies from a mean line would for the most part amount to "less than the breadth of a London square." Even before hearing formally from the Astronomer Royal, Lord Derby cabled Captain Cameron, March 27: "Do not take any steps for tracing mean boundary until you receive further instructions from me."

Meanwhile at Dufferin the winter passed quite peacefully. In December no outdoor work went on except hauling firewood and drawing hay from meadows where it had been stacked during the summer. There was sufficient snow for sleighing, but only thirty or forty horses remained at work, the rest being allowed to ramble about unshod during the day. Snowdrifts would soon bury the stables and keep them warm. Invitations came for a Christmas ball at the Governor's house in Fort Garry. In January Captain Anderson began planning the next season's operations, which would involve a 460-mile advance before any survey work could begin, and an 850-mile retreat in the fall. Pack animals would be necessary in the vicinity of the Rocky Mountains; there would be more Indians to deal with; and hay must be stacked at twenty-mile intervals along the last 450 miles of the return route against destruction of the natural forage by fire. Veterinary Boswell was sent to the States to arrange delivery of oats from Missouri River ports like Fort Benton. Plans were even made for a party of fifty men to winter near the Rockies should the work remain unfinished.

With his wife away, Captain Cameron moved into the officers' barracks, but his presence irritated Captain Anderson, who complained in letters home of not being able to get decisions. When the Commissioner left for Ottawa in February, his chief astronomer wrote, "I felt rather sorry for Captain C. for while he was here he invited nobody's confidence, never got up till eleven, shut himself up in his room all day, never went out, and we saw nothing of him except at meals. Being a very obstinate man, his obstinacy was allowed to run its course, and I found it quite impossible to do any business with him except on paper."

Quite unconsciously Captain Anderson revealed his own philosophy and tireless energy in describing a sled dog which he had befriended and allowed to sleep in his room: "My dog had to go away a few days ago in a train with three others to the Lake of the Woods, and my room feels very lonely without him. He is far too eager in harness and does most of the work, pulling at his little collar continuously, while the lazy dogs before and behind him take it easy. It becomes necessary to thrash the lazy dogs occasionally in order to spare the willing ones."

At the end of February the three officers remaining in the headquarters mess gave a ball for their neighbors at Fort Pembina. Eight couples in kid gloves and full dress came to dance quadrilles to the music of a brass band from Fort Garry. Mrs. Herchmer and Mrs. Almon, the wife of the farm superintendent, prepared a splendid supper. The party lasted from 8 P. M. until three-thirty the next morning. Captain Anderson quoted one of the American officers as saying, late in the evening and in the fullness of his heart: "You Britishers know how to do the thing in proper style." Pleased as he was by this remark, Anderson could not resist coupling it with a comment of his own on the lack of freshness in his neighbors' complexions: "This state of things among Americans is not to be wondered at when you consider that they live in heated houses, on a diet of pickles and candies, and gobble their food at such a rate that it has been calculated that the average time an American takes for his dinner is six and a half minutes."

In reciprocity the American officers at Fort Pembina entertained the British contingent a month later. Five of the latter, including the two ladies, sleighed over on the ice of the river, the snow being gone from the road. A party of two dozen danced to the music of a banjo and violin from nine until midnight. Then there was a snake dance, in and out around the supper tables, before the company sat down. Captain Anderson may have revised his notions about the American diet because he mentioned fried oysters, chicken salad, turkey and hams; then ice cream, "a great American dish," cake, almonds, raisins and coffee. After supper there was "the German Dance," with a peculiar headdress or ornament issued to each person for every figure. "There were two immense basket-fulls of these fancy ornaments which had been procured from New York for the occasion . . . I brought away a wreathe and a pair of pantomime spectacles."

While the British were snug in winter quarters, Lieutenant Greene was occupied checking their tangent lines from the Red River fifty-six miles eastward, and completing the topographical survey south of the parallel. With him he had three civilian assistants, Orrin S. Wilson, Charles L. Doolittle and Alfred Downing, and about fifty hired men, including eight teamsters and seven dog drivers. Greene used six-mule teams rather than oxen to freight his supplies on sledges to Point d'Orme, thirty-three miles from Pembina, where he stocked a depot. On the ice of Roseau River and Lake the mules could go as far as Pine River. Farther eastward, and over the frozen swamps, dog trains were employed. By November 20,

Greene had run the tangent to West Roseau and a week later to Point d'Orme. In the subzero weather beef had to be sawed off in slabs and frozen vinegar chopped out with a hatchet. Eggs could not be opened to be fried—boiling was the only way to cook them. The men wore havelocks made of blanket, buffalo-hide coats and trousers, and moose-leather mittens and moccasins.

On December 15th the American tangent line reached Pine River station, fifty-six miles from Red River, where Lieutenant Galwey, coming west from the Lake of the Woods the previous winter, had discontinued marking the parallel. Lieutenant Greene wrote that, running his tangent lines through the British cuttings and taking his own observations, the work closed on theirs without any appreciable discrepancy—the differences being only a foot or a few inches. He therefore marked the parallel every mile for fifty-six miles east of Red River, and cut it out to a width of ten feet. This was tacit acceptance of the corrections proposed by the British the winter before.

At the end of December Greene embarked on a trip to the mouth of the Rainy River, in connection with a survey of the lake shore south of the parallel. Here he found an Indian village, the inhabitants of which were much disturbed by his arrival. "One man came into camp about an hour before dark, sat around the fire for two or three hours and then informed us that he had something to say but as it was getting late he would come and say it in the morning." Returning the next day with a chief and several others, the same individual announced, after much pipe-smoking and questioning as to Greene's purpose, that the land belonged to the Indians, that they had made no treaties with the Government and wanted none, that they did not wish the land surveyed, and finally that "he

was starving and would be glad to receive some rations."
Greene refused to provide any food, upon which the Indians said that the "Shakanese (English) always gave them
more than the Chomokoman (Americans) but that all
parties coming here had given them something."

X

SECOND SORTIE

LIEUTENANT GREENE returned to Fort Pembina at the end of January, 1874. From then on, except for another trip by D'Arcy East to the Lake of the Woods, there was no surveying until after the spring break-up. Just before this occurred all the officers on leave returned to Dufferin, and with them Captain Cameron. In a sudden economy move he reduced the hired men's daily allowance of meat from 1½ lbs. to 1 lb., and when thirty-three of the oldest employees protested, he ordered them discharged. This event greatly distressed Captain Anderson who, equities aside, dreaded starting the long march west with untried men. His own relations with the British Commissioner deteriorated further when a letter arrived from the Astronomer Royal in answer to one Anderson had written, confirming the view that a mean parallel was unnecessary. Anderson showed the letter to

Cameron and recorded the reaction: "Capt. C. is now very indignant with me that I should have written to the Astronomer Royal, the whole sting lying in the fact that Capt. C. will have to follow the advice which I gave him nearly two years ago and which he has been resisting ever since."

The first steamboat arrived at Dufferin on April 28, before the new grass began to sprout. Nevertheless on May 2 a party of scouts and axemen under the leadership of Mr. Crompton set out for Woody Mountain and Lieutenant Rowe took a group of Royal Engineers into the field to prepare the roads and bridge the creeks for the supply trains. Even earlier, on April 22, Dr. Millman had left Dufferin for Pembina Mountain depot with Sergeant Major Flower and an ox-team. The doctor noted, "no butter and no cheese on the line this summer; meat consists of one pound of bacon per day per man . . . fortunately game is plentiful, prairie chickens, ducks and geese." Their camp was threatened by a prairie fire burning in the old grass; to avoid it they moved the tents across a coulée.

Conditioning themselves for the march, the chief astronomer's party and the two parties under Featherstonhaugh and Galwey camped out on the prairie near the barracks. Featherstonhaugh again had with him subastronomer King, while Mr. Carvell served as computer. His Royal Engineers assistants, whom he commended by name at the end of the season, were Corporal Drew, Lance Corporal Quint and Sappers Curtis, Parsons and Jewel. Subastronomers Burpee and Coster accompanied Galwey, Corporal Lovell being the senior Royal Engineers assistant.

Captain Anderson, impatiently awaiting an ox-train of

fifty wagons coming up from Minnesota at ten miles a day, commented that the resort to such transport had been "conceived very much in the same spirit that Buonaparte planned his march to Moscow, using oxen and remarking that 'when the army can no longer nourish the oxen, the oxen can be made to nourish the army.' " Anderson favored using horses and carts exclusively to haul supplies, but was overruled. He shared his camp with Dawson the geologist, whose assistant kept the table supplied with ducks. Their cook stuttered and did his work the better for being able only to whistle at it.

On May 20, the day that the main expedition of eleven officers and 128 men finally left Dufferin, Lieutenant Rowe's party, meanwhile joined by Dr. Millman and an advance train of twenty ox-drawn wagons, reached Turtle Mountain. There they found, quite secure, the two keepers who had been left behind to guard the depot during the winter. One of them, George Arthur Hill, had been charged by Captain Cameron with learning the intentions of the Sioux. He reported only thirty-six Indians in seven lodges wintering at the mountain, although their chiefs represented larger groups who visited in the spring from Portage La Prairie to trap muskrat and mink. The intelligence obtained by Hill was reassuring in that it related to the anxiety of the Indians about being handed over to the Americans, rather than to feelings of hostility toward the surveyors. Nevertheless, a report of a hostile combination of tribes reached Ottawa and, transmitted back to Cameron in garbled form, caused some apprehension later.

Instructions issued by the Commissioner in May, 1874, reflected the directive of the previous spring from the Foreign Office regarding Indians: "Should any hindrance

to the progress of the various parties be offered by Indians," read the instructions, "no force must be used to
remove the hindrance," but the circumstance communicated without delay to headquarters and to the other
parties on the line. Furthermore, "should the Indians assume a decided objection to the progress of the expedition, the parties will return toward Dufferin," endeavor-
ing, however, "if possible to do so without causing an
open rupture," to remain where they were until those
ahead had been given a chance to retreat. Fortunately
this directive, the language of which left much room
for interpretation, never had to be implemented on the
way west. Situations where its strict observance might
have paralyzed all activity are not difficult to imagine.

At the end of May Crompton and his scouts arrived at
Woody Mountain and commenced the construction of a
depot. Crompton's next move was a reconnaissance westward, beyond the site of the first British astronomical station for 1874, to explore Frenchman's Creek. This stream,
also known as the White Mud River, crossed the parallel
in a deep gorge. Crompton had to go north sixteen miles
to find a place where vehicles could pass on the hunters'
track from Woody Mountain to Fort Benton. Some distance beyond this crossing he located the site for a second
astronomical station on Cottonwood Coulée, 479 miles
west of Red River. Near the crossing itself, sixty-nine
miles by road from Woody Mountain, a place for a subdepot was also selected.

Captain Anderson and the main supply train overtook
Lieutenant Rowe near the first crossing of the Souris
River, where high water at the usual ford made necessary the construction of a bridge. Once over this, the 100-
wagon train advanced to Wood End, where the astro-

nomical parties detached themselves to travel with the horse-drawn transport directly through the Coteau to their initial stations. Anderson, with the slower ox-teams, would proceed by the traders' road northwestward toward Woody Mountain. At this juncture an unfortunate accident befell Lieutenant Rowe, incapacitating him for the rest of the summer. At a gallop, his horse stepped into a badger hole and threw him off. Landing on his head, Rowe suffered a fracture at the base of his skull and for a time loss of his senses. Captain Ward and Dr. Burgess remained with him, establishing a hospital camp on the prairie where he fell. There he remained for several weeks until he could be moved to Wood End depot. At first it was thought that, when able, Rowe should go back to Dufferin in an ambulance and then to New York or London for treatment, the sergeant major being assigned to escort him. But by August he had recovered sufficiently to proceed to the depot at Woody Mountain, whence he returned with the others in the fall. Rowe was greatly esteemed by his fellows, Captain Anderson describing him as "a most accomplished officer and a magnificent fellow for work."

Mr. Ashe, who had been Rowe's assistant, took over the topographical party and proceeded through the Coteau to begin work beyond West Poplar Creek. With him Ashe had Sergeant Kay as senior Royal Engineer and Corporal Malings, Lance Corporal Maule and Sapper McNicol as topographers. The zone for topographical survey north of the parallel was reduced in 1874 to a width of three miles, except at the western end of the line.

Captain Featherstonhaugh reached his station, Little Rocky Creek (432 miles west), on June 20, Lieutenant Galwey commencing observations at Cottonwood Coulée

four days later. Meanwhile Captain Anderson arrived,
June 22, at the new depot at Woody Mountain, 460 miles
by road from Dufferin, in thirty-two days' march, including six of halts. He was relieved to find there sixty tons
of oats, freighted in by a contractor from Fort Benton
without escort. Dr. Millman, summoned from Featherstonhaugh's camp to Woody Mountain to attend Sapper
McCammon, who had just shot himself the second time,
described the place as consisting of "hills quite destitute
of woods but the latter abound in the valleys and coulées.
A beautiful stream of water runs north through it. There
appears to be quite a settlement here of half-breeds, most
of whom are away at present near Cypress Hills hunting."

The day after Captain Anderson's arrival Mr. Crompton and six scouts left Woody Mountain on a second reconnaissance, while a train of wagons started out to stock
the depot at White Mud crossing. Mr. Crompton explored 150 miles west to the East Fork of the Milk River,
where on July 7 Anderson and Herchmer would set up
a second subdepot. Before this expedition the chief astronomer visited his working parties on the line south of
Woody Mountain and made contact with an American
scout from Fort Peck. His appearance heralded the coming of the American Commission, who, instead of marching five hundred miles along the parallel, were able, as
Lieutenant Galwey enviously put it, to "travel like gentlemen by steamer up the Missouri."

Because Congress delayed renewing its appropriation
for the boundary survey until the beginning of June, the
Americans were very late setting out. Major Twining saw
Captain Cameron on June 3 in St. Paul, where a discussion of the astronomical parallel took place. The
next day, on learning of the imminent passage of the ap-

Métis Family Group and Camp
Note Red River Carts

Int. Boundary Comm.

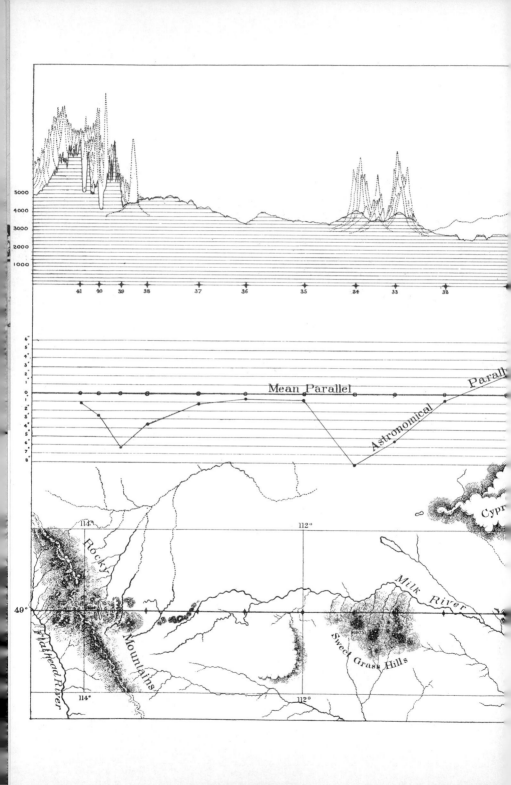

Sergeant Kay's Survey Party ABOVE
Note Water Cart and Camera

Pub. Archives Canada

Diagram of Relative Errors in Latitude, Mean and Astronomical
Parallels AT LEFT

1878 Report

U.S.N.B. SURVEY.
Marching upon the West Roseau River, from Point d'Orme
on the way to Pine River and Ridge. December 16. 1873.

Sketch by Alfred Downing
New York Public Library

propriation bill, the American chief astronomer started
for Bismarck, his parties having already been organized
and the transport train sent ahead. The rail journey
proved no hardship for the officers, who were invited to
ride in the official car of the Northern Pacific's superintendent. At the railhead on the Missouri River, Twining
found the steamer *Fontenelle* waiting, but already loaded
with two hundred tons of non-Commission freight. This
with his own wagons and animals would cram the boat
to capacity for the week's passage to Fort Buford. Before
departure, June 7, Lieutenant Greene wrote to his parents: "About the 20th of this month Custer takes ten companies of cavalry—about 500 effective men—and starts
on an expedition southwest into the Black Hills. The Indians are collecting down there in large numbers to op-
pose him and he will probably have some hard fighting,
but he has a fine regiment of several years' experience
with Indians and as an Indian fighter Custer has no superior in the Army except Mackenzie. His expedition
will benefit us by drawing the Indians away from our
scene of operations."

Greene described the *Fontenelle* as a stern-wheeler
two hundred feet in length, thirty in the beam, with accommodations for twenty cabin passengers. "Everything
above the hull is built like all these western river boats—
of ½ inch and inch pine and the decks shake with the
motion of the boat like so much paper." On board the
Commission had 140 animals, 110 men, 38 wagons and
270 tons of property and stores. The horses and mules
were in two pens on the lower deck, thirty by forty feet,
packed in so close they couldn't kick. Fresh hay was
thrown on them, and each animal in turn got pushed by
the others to the feed boxes on the sides, and watered the

same way. The officers and assistants lived in the cabins, the men in the dismounted wagons or on deck, where a couple of stoves were set up and rations cooked. The Commission paid $4,300 for its passage of 385 miles upstream, the boat moving against the current only about seventy-five miles in a day of twenty hours. Daily consumption of fuel to feed its three boilers came to twenty cords, purchased from woodcutters along the banks at five dollars a cord.

When after five days hay ran short, Major Twining landed the mules at the Tobacco Garden, to be herded overland the rest of the way to Fort Buford. There they arrived on June 15, a few hours behind the boat and a day after the cavalry escort coming from Fort Totten. This season the American Commission would have with it five companies of the 6th Infantry and two of the 7th Cavalry, all under the command of Major Reno. The cavalry companies were the same as before; Captain Weir had Company D but Captain Keogh was abroad on leave, leaving the command of Company I to Lieutenant Porter, who also served as adjutant of the escort. Lieutenant Greene described the scene at the fort: "A large post, with garrison of six companies, on the plain under the bluff near the river . . . up on the bluff are the pickets (Indian scouts) and around the post are camped between 500 and 600 men, and herds grazing near the hills of 200 horses, 500 mules and 200 beef cattle. And all this to find a line, which doubtless the framers of the Treaty imagined would be the most simple and economical boundary ever agreed upon!"

After a few days' layover at Fort Buford, resting and shoeing the animals, the expedition set out on June 21 to follow the north bank of the Missouri as far as the

Poplar River, where a separation would take place. The mouth of Big Muddy Creek was found impassable for the train of 110 wagons, so in a day and a half Lieutenant Greene energetically threw over a bridge. On the twenty-sixth, at the Poplar, Greene's contingent of about seventy men, with its escort of Companies E and I, 6th Infantry, under Captain Edwin R. Ames, and thirteen Indian scouts, left the main column. Greene followed the stream northward until it forked. There he detached two topographical parties under Charles L. Doolittle and Dr. Valentine T. McGillycuddy to reconnoiter the west fork, while his tangent party and a third group of topographers under Orrin S. Wilson explored the east. This brought him on June 29 to the point on the parallel 385 miles from Red River, where his topographical survey had ended the previous season.

Captain Gregory, with his astronomical party and assistants Lewis Boss and Addison J. Edgerton, continued with the main column past the mouth of the Milk River to a point on its north bank opposite an old trading post called "Tom Campbell's Houses." There he diverged, July 2, crossing Little Rocky Creek and then the gulch of Frenchman's Creek below a trading post called Fort N.J. Turnay. This log stockade was occupied by two traders whose horses had been run off by a party of Uncpapa Sioux the day before Gregory's arrival. He left the trading post on July 5 and after a northward march of twenty-five miles in intense heat found water in a pool at the boundary. This point to the west of Frenchman's Creek and 462 miles from Red River would be his first astronomical station for 1874.

Attached to Captain Gregory's party were Dr. Elliott Coues, assistant army surgeon and naturalist of the American Commission; an escort of forty men of Company D, 6th Infantry, commanded by Captain Montgomery Bryant; three Indians and a white scout named George Boyd. Besides his two assistants, Gregory had a foreman, two cooks, a waiter, five hands and six teamsters. Transport for the surveying instruments and a month's supply of provender comprised a four-mule spring wagon, three six-mule army wagons, and two Minnesota wagons drawn by pairs of mules. Gregory himself rode horseback, and a horse and buckboard were provided for Dr. Coues.

Thus by rail, steamboat and wagon train the Americans reached their initial stations on the parallel approximately a month after leaving St. Paul. It took them about the same length of time as the British march from Dufferin, but they arrived on the line ten days to two weeks later.

XI

ON THE MILK RIVER
WATERSHED

WHILE his astronomical and tangent parties were following side creeks northward to the line, Major Twining, with the main supply train and the cavalry escort, continued up the Milk River road past Fort Belknap to Sandy or Box Elder Creek. Here, about forty-five miles from Fort Benton, a temporary base was established, and the chief astronomer and Major Reno rode over to the Missouri to find out what had become of a contract train supposed to meet them with more forage. At Fort Benton they discovered the train waiting on demurrage, but the steamboat *Josephine,* bringing the supplies from Bismarck, not yet arrived. She finally appeared on July 22, bringing only twenty-five tons of corn, having left twice that amount, because of low water, at Cow Island, 120 miles downstream. Twining despatched a train to fetch part of this, and another to take the twenty-five tons of corn to the Sweet Grass Hills, where the American Cavalry base was established, August 1, at the East Butte. The two remaining infantry companies guarded these trains, since the cavalry was designed as a compact striking force "to punish at once any large demonstrations of the Indians," as Lieutenant Greene put it.

On approaching the parallel Greene's party had seen every day large numbers of antelope, whose curiosity brought them right up to the tents at times of quiet. On July 12 he wrote from a point 500 miles west of Red River, Captain Gregory's second astronomical station, that his scouts had killed two buffalo: "There are a dozen of these Indian scouts in my part of the escort, with an Irish half-breed, Val Wheeler, at the head who talks French and English well beside six Indian languages. These scouts represent the Gros Ventres, Arickarees and Assiniboines. They are enlisted for six months and receive the pay and allowances of cavalry soldiers and so much per day for furnishing their own pony and saddle. On the march they drive the beef herd and in camp are posted as pickets on the hills around camp, and occasionally are sent ahead to find out about the country. Their dress was originally a uniform, but is now somewhat changed, the pantaloons being cut away into leggings reaching to the thigh and a breech clout inserted under the blouse; beads on the clothes and brass in the braids of the hair, ears, fingers, etc., and paint on the cheeks according to the taste of the wearer."

Gregory and Greene made great efforts to catch up with the British, who were still a station ahead of them in mid-July. Captain Featherstonhaugh, after finishing at Little Rocky Creek, moved on to Goose Lake, 527 miles west, and Lieutenant Galwey to the West Fork of the Milk

River, 567 miles from Red River. Featherstonhaugh was the first to meet Indians; on July 11 at his second station he encountered a band of Assiniboines who were given a present of bacon, flour and tea. According to Dr. Millman, "they appeared to be very friendly. There were about thirty all mounted on very good ponies and well armed. Some had Winchester repeaters or sixteen shooters." The next day the Indians moved their camp near to the surveyors and Dr. Millman counted sixty tepees. "The Indians are making great slaughter amongst the geese on the lake as they are now not able to fly, having shed their feathers."

Captain Featherstonhaugh found his visitors "particularly keen after matches"; he was unaware that they used the heads as a substitute for fulminate in reloading rimfire cartridges for their Winchesters. They asked him numerous questions about the expedition and appeared relieved that no idea of a railway lay at the bottom of it. A marked boundary separating the United States from the "grandmother country" seemed welcome, the Indians being only disappointed it would not be "a wall or continuous bank across the plains." While the British party was still at Goose Lake, Lieutenant Greene came up, running the tangent from Captain Gregory's second station at the 500-mile point. Dr. Millman called at his camp and met the officers of the infantry escort, Captain Ames, Lieutenants Crowell, Walker and Murdoch and Dr. Lord.

No doubt the conversation turned to buffalo running, which Greene and his escort commander had engaged in for the first time a day or so before. "It is the wildest and grandest sport I ever saw or engaged in," wrote Greene. Sighting a large dark cloud of animals moving over the horizon, whose "peculiar clumsy rolling lope" could be made out through the transit telescope, he had his horse saddled and rode out from camp with Captain Ames and two scouts. A turn around a hill brought them less than a quarter of a mile from a band of eighty buffalo quietly grazing, a few old bulls on the outside around others in a clump. "The old bull in front soon saw us and with a snort threw down his head and up his tail and started off; the herd looked around at us, threw down their heads and rolled after him—and away we went. It seemed at first a slow lumbering gait like a lot of black cows frightened by a dog, but we soon found out that they were going a good 12 or 15 miles an hour with lots of wind inside their black hides." Galloping up to within fifty feet, the Indian scout shot two cows while Greene, emptying his revolver, wounded a bull. This Val Wheeler, the head scout, finished off. Ames managed to crease his own horse in the leg with a revolver bullet, earning Greene's caustic comment: "Evidently the looking after horse, self, rifle, pistol, buffalo and badger holes at a gallop had been too much for him—an Infantry man."

Captain Anderson was meanwhile ahead of all the parties, reconnoitering with D'Arcy East. The latter had succeeded to the command of the 49th Rangers, with Crompton as deputy, following Hallett's death during the winter. Anderson met no Indians, noting rather disappointedly, "Galwey and Featherstonhaugh have had to do all the shaking of hands." After exploring the Milk River gorge to find a crossing for wagons, the only favorable spot lying ten miles south of the parallel, the reconnaissance continued to the East Butte of the Sweet Grass Hills, where Anderson turned back. Crompton went on to locate another depot at the West Butte, which would also become

Lieutenant Galwey's third astronomical station, 651 miles from Red River.

While bringing up supplies to West Butte, Anderson narrowly escaped a buffalo stampede. He wrote that as the train was crossing a small ravine east of the Milk River "the buffalo, extended over the plains for many miles, took fright and all rushed toward us and were drawn into the little ravine as into a funnel. I was afraid our horses and wagons would be swept away, but we were able to stop in time, and thousands of the terrified buffalo swept past us just in front, smothering us with dust. It was no good firing into the midst of them, although they were quite close, 50 yards off, so we waited 10 minutes till they had all passed." The buffalo charged through the only pool of water in sight for miles, so that the horses would scarcely drink of it.

With no rain for over three weeks the Milk River had stopped running, while locusts devoured nearly all the remaining grass. These insects were known as "Mormon crickets," of a blackish brown color, an inch and a half long. Dawson had first encountered them in June in the Great Coteau where the ground for twenty miles was covered with young grasshoppers not yet able to fly. He believed that they hatched out where flights of the previous season had rested. At Frenchman's Creek on July 12 swarms were observed taking to wing and "causing a noise like that of the distant sound of surf, or a gentle breeze among pine trees." Eighteen seventy-four was a bad year for locusts on the western plains, just as 1818, 1857, and 1868 had been.

On this same journey Anderson came upon a camp of Métis hunters. Their tents and Red River carts were arranged in two concentric circles so as to make a horse corral at night. "They had a band of about 500 horses," wrote Anderson, "which were let loose and grazed round the camp during the day, protected by two lines of mounted scouts who kept the animals from straying. These people had camped near the buffalo and killed about 200, and had preserved the meat by cutting it in slices and drying it. Many of the families had no other food but this meat. They are semi-civilized, all speak French, and a priest travels with them." The chief astronomer hired half a dozen of the hunters who knew the country west and could speak Blackfoot to join his party. In this camp Dr. Dawson counted two hundred tepees, mostly of buffalo hide but some of canvas. The Métis, he learned, had recently come from the Cypress Hills, where they had assisted or countenanced the Sioux in a fight with the Blackfeet.

Captain Gregory commenced observations at his third station, the East Fork of the Milk River, 553 miles from Red River, on July 15. He reached Milk River Lake, 588 miles west, a week later, just as Captain Featherstonhaugh began his third station, beyond the Milk River crossing, 614 miles west. Here the sight of large herds of buffalo tempted Dr. Millman and the British captain to ride out and run them. Still a station behind, however, Gregory lacked time for such pursuits.

With Lieutenant Greene's party running the tangent to the next station, work that the British astronomers had to do themselves, the American astronomer caught up with his opposite numbers at the Sweet Grass Hills. There at the beginning of August a great concentration took place—with the United States cavalry based at the East Butte and the British main depot at the West, whither Major Twining moved his camp, August 2. Commissary

Herchmer and a single companion rode seventy-two miles in to Fort Benton to arrange the delivery of a contract train of oats. Lieutenant Galwey completed his fix at West Butte just as Captain Gregory approached to observe his fifth station near the cavalry camp, where there was a fine spring of pure cold water. Here Lieutenant Greene arrived on July 31, having for ten days left his escort behind with the topographical parties. This was the result of an order issued by Major Reno that Captain Ames should not separate himself from his detachments by more than forty miles. Such constraint, imposed without consulting the engineer being escorted, would have delayed Greene, whose tangent party was always in a race to keep up with the astronomers. Hence, not wishing the tail to wag the dog, he had set out without escort.

In the buffalo country between Goose Lake and the Milk River crossing Greene's party had encountered an Assiniboine band, who visited his camp asking something to eat. These Indians also wanted to know if a railroad was being built. Captain Ames explained the object of the expedition but gave out no presents. Dr. McGilly-cuddy's topographers received several equivocal visits from some Sioux. On July 25, after joining forces with Doolittle, the doctor noted in his diary that "25 Yanktons, Deer Tail Chief, came down on us from the hills but seeing our numbers had been reinforced by Sergeant Litchfield, four men and a blacksmith, he finally left us. In the afternoon [our party] was overtaken by a half-breed and 8 Yanktons and Assiniboines who also left us." This attention was probably motivated more by curiosity than hostility, but the surveyors could not be sure. A few days before a scout bringing the mail from Fort Belknap had been chased into camp by Indians.

Lieutenant Greene noticed that the plains west of Goose Lake became poorer and poorer. "I sometimes wonder," he wrote, "if the original geographer who left an immense blank in the middle of the map of America and labelled it 'Great American Desert' was so far wrong." Grazing for his animals could seldom be found; he passed long patches of bluish clay in which only a microscopic sagebrush grew and other stretches of whitish clay with nothing but cactus. There still remained enough pools of surface water to supply his camps but the streams feeding the Milk River had run dry. In its precipitous gorge Greene observed "a small collection of log huts, said to be those of Piegans—also some fine black-tailed deer and numerous rattlesnakes, of a greenish color, about 4 feet long, 1½ inches in diameter at the largest and with 3 to 7 rattles."

The concentration at the Sweet Grass Hills afforded an appropriate moment for the two boundary Commissioners to make their appearance. Captain Cameron, driving a buckboard out along the boundary trail, arrived at West Butte on July 25; after recalling Captain Anderson from a reconnaissance toward the end of the line, he set out with two scouts for that objective himself. Commissioner Campbell meanwhile reached East Butte, August 2, following an uneventful march of seventeen days from Fort Buford. He was accompanied by secretary Bangs and escorted by Lieutenant T.G. Townshend and fifteen men from Company D of the 6th Infantry. Soon afterward Dr. Coues, traveling this season with Captain Gregory's party, was joined by a professional taxidermist, Joseph H. Batty.

While Dr. Coues concentrated on birds, particularly Swainson's buzzard and other hawks found nesting in the cutbanks of the Milk River and feeding on gophers, Batty pursued antelope and buffalo. Writing from the Sweet Grass Hills, August 8, he mentioned that "several old bulls have been seen by our party, and were chased by a mob composed of teamsters and cooks mounted on mules." While one bull was actually overtaken in this fashion and wounded, the hunt produced no meat. Batty observed numerous skeletons of huge bulls, and occasionally one of a cow, killed by Indians for lodge skins. "They dress their game 'Indian fashion,' simply unjointing the legs from the body and stripping the flesh from the carcass in thin pieces for drying. The larger bones are cracked, boiled in a large camp kettle, and the marrow skimmed for making pemmican." Batty stalked a great many mountain sheep and one evening with a Sharps rifle shot an old ram, having to "sleep all night alongside of the meat so as to keep my share from the wolves."

At the Buttes Dr. Coues found no avian specialties but observed numerous mountain sheep and yellow-haired porcupines. One or more golden eagles was frequently in sight, their nests being "composed of sticks, some as large as a man's wrist, brushwood and bunches of grass and weeds with masses of earth still adhering to the roots." Dr. Coues considered the Milk River region the center of prairie gopher abundance, where they lived one gopher to a hole, feeding on the carcasses of buffalo. In turn, the gophers attracted rattlesnakes.

While no live Indians were seen near the Sweet Grass Hills by either the British or the Americans, the cavalry camp was rife with "many rumors of anticipated troubles," to quote the report of Major Reno. Accordingly, on August 6, the day that the assembled American Commission had its picture taken by courtesy of the Royal Engineers photographers at West Butte, the cavalry commander set out on a scout to the end of the line. "I went to within 50 miles of the western limit of the work, passing through many Indians, but all were friendly and were hunting or going to their hunting grounds and had with them their villages, lodge poles, women and children, and showed permits from their different agents; they were Blackfeet and Piegans mostly."

Reno turned back, August 9, at the North Branch of the Milk River, to which point, 716 miles west, Captain Featherstonhaugh's party had just completed the tangent from the South Branch (697 miles west). At the last-mentioned place, also called the second Milk River crossing, Featherstonhaugh had been observing since August 2. Dr. Millman's entry of this date confirmed the peaceful character of the Indians in the vicinity: "We saw some Blackfoot Indians. They appear to be very friendly. All they ask is that we wipe those whiskey traders out of existence, for they are robbing them—getting all their ponies, etc." On August 8, he noted: "Saw about one hundred of the North Piegan Indians—very poorly clad. They were quite friendly and two or three had credentials. They were to the effect that they were going north to join their tribe—good Indians, etc. One of them had an English Testament with the name of John Sinclair in it. He also had a book of sermons in French." On the next day the observant young doctor wrote: "Some of the American cavalry arrived in the morning, having heard that the Indians were collecting in this neighborhood. On learning to the contrary, they went back to the Buttes."

The three buttes comprising the Sweet Grass Hills each consisted of a cluster of foothills lying around a central peak or peaks, the summits of which rose some thirty-five hundred feet above the eastward plains and nearly seven thousand feet above sea level. Often a shower of rain or hail fell in the afternoon and the buttes gave rise to numerous little brooks and rivulets which ran at night and dried up in the daytime. These nourished the lush grass around the base of the hills where an occasional grove of quaking aspens could bc found. "Most of this grass is very nutritious," wrote Lieutenant Greene, "but some of it is very distasteful to animals, having a peculiar rounded stem, a sweetish taste like sugar cane and a peculiar odor; hence the name Sweet Grass Hills." On their upper slopes only stunted pine and cedars grew, many of the larger trees dead or fallen, with evidences of fire. The wood provided a welcome alternative to the buffalo chips that the surveyors had been cooking with on the treeless plains.

XII

THE END OF THE LINE

WHILE the British parties pushed on ahead, the Americans spent a few days at the West Butte shoeing their horses and mules and resetting wagon tires. Commissioner Campbell, his sixty-one years notwithstanding, rode to the top of the butte with Lieutenant Greene to get a magnificant view of the Rocky Mountains rising from the plain a hundred miles away. Dr. McGillycuddy "topoged" the vicinity, and one afternoon visited a recent battleground where the remains of twenty or more Indians had been found. His diary recorded that he "got three pairs of femurs, one head and one infer max." The dead belonged to the Crow tribe and were thought to have been caught by the Piegans during a horse-stealing raid, before they could reach the shelter of the buttes. Captain Anderson, who came upon the bodies earlier, wrote that they were "all sun dried and features distinguishable. Every head had the whole of the hair removed in the Indian process of scalping, and there were empty cartridges and arrowheads lying on all sides." The victims had made some resistance in pits hastily dug with knives and Anderson surmised "that when they had all been killed their conquerors collected the bodies together and had a war dance round them." Dawson the geologist arranged for some photographs to be taken.

Captain Gregory left West Butte, August 6, to observe at Red Creek, 672 miles west, near where the Whoop-up Trail from Fort Benton crossed the parallel to the Saskatchewan whiskey-trading posts. Thence he went to the North Branch of the Milk River, where Major Reno had turned back from his scout. Lieutenant Galwey was by now at his fourth and last station, the crossing of the St. Mary's River, 737 miles from Red River, where East and Crompton had found a camp of friendly Blackfeet and located the last depot, called Rocky Mountains. When this depot was stocked, the slow moving ox-train, in charge of Hugh O'Donnell, started on the back trail.

Captain Cameron did not reach the 1861 monument at the end of the line, although he attempted to do so with pack animals until they were frightened by a grizzly bear. Captain Anderson met him returning and found him quite touchy and fault-finding. Their brief conference at the last depot ended without disagreement, but two days later on a further reconnaissance the chief astronomer was overtaken by an order to cut down the daily meat ration for each man from 1½ lbs. to 1 lb. During the summer the cut of the previous spring had been restored. Possibly the reduction was again intended as an economy move, although there could be little object in driving any of the beef herd back to Dufferin. Unable to protest because the

British Commissioner was already en route for Red River,
Anderson expressed his distaste in a letter home: "If anything could be calculated to cause mutiny and trouble
among our working parties it is a vexatious reduction of
their allowance of food. The reduction now ordered is
the work of a madman, as our cattle having made a journey of 800 miles are not fat and the principal portion of
the ration of beef is bone."

Captain Cameron's irritability perhaps stemmed from
the fact that at last he would have to eat humble pie before his opposite number, the American Commissioner.
The Foreign Office had finally instructed him not only to
accept the Indians' site for the reference monument at
the northwest point but also to agree to an astronomical
instead of a mean parallel along 49 degrees north. With
the last instruction came an opinion from the Astronomer
Royal, saying that the boundary ought to be determined
solely by considerations of astronomical latitude. The
local variations of course averaged out and the extreme
discrepancies, occurring at three astronomical stations toward the western end of the line, came to 600 feet north
and 600 and 800 feet south of the calculated mean. Nowhere else did they exceed 350 feet in either direction.
At the Red River Valley, the only settled portion of the
line, adoption of a mean parallel could have moved the
boundary some 300 feet south.

The day of reckoning had arrived, so on August 13,
when Commissioner Campbell was camped with Major
Twining on the South Branch of the Milk River, Captain
Cameron "unexpectedly made his appearance among us."
His far from conciliatory surrender was embodied in a
letter, which stated on the main point in dispute: "Provided it be understood that the determinations at astro-

nomical stations be accepted however the results may indicate discrepancies between neighboring stations, and that the line between these astronomically determined points shall follow a course *having the uniform curvature of a parallel of 49° of north latitude,* I shall agree to your proposal to determine the line by independent astronomical observation at successive points."

The italics in the above quotation have been supplied to emphasize how the letter, which Campbell accepted, differed from the precedent established in the 1869 agreement relating to the boundary west of the Rockies. There the line between any two monuments was defined as a "right or straight line," whereas east of the Rockies it would curve. The difference did not amount to much with monuments even three miles apart, but it would still pose a problem later for local surveyors. Had Anderson been consulted or included in the meeting at Milk River, or the Astronomer Royal's sanction of a straight line regarded, this technical defect might have been obviated. As it was, the British Commissioner, in determined pursuit of a curved line, wrote a stipulation that could only be corrected by subsequent treaty.

The Milk River Ridge, skirting the North Fork of that river to the northwest, marked a divide between Missouri waters and those flowing to Hudson's Bay. The boundary crossed the ridge 720 miles from Red River at an altitude of forty-seven hundred feet. Beyond, at the crossing of the St. Mary's River, the character of the land changed to a hilly district of thick timber and underbrush. Lieutenant Galwey ran his tangent line only part way to the Belly River crossing (748 miles west). This, as Captain Featherstonhaugh's last station, was sited five miles north of the parallel because the latter at that point was inaccessible to wagon transport. Connection with Galwey's tangent was made by triangulation. The same method served to join the Belly River station with the parallel and over Mount Wilson to Captain Gregory's last fix on the west side of Waterton Lake (759 miles west). Between the latter and the 1861 monument (765 miles from Red River), the longitude was determined by traversing up the Kootenay Pass. This work occupied the last two weeks in August and was shared by both Commissions, who camped at the lake side by side.

Captain Anderson was the first to reach the monument erected in 1861. Having tried without success to find a direct route through the mountainous ravines, he took to the Kootenay Indian Trail from the northern end of Waterton Lake, crossing the summit of the continental range at seventy-one hundred feet above sea level. Camp was made, August 16, on the western side of the divide at a point where the trail of the previous survey branched off to the monument. Anderson had with him Crompton and Dawson and six axmen with pack horses. The old track on which the blazes still showed distinctly was choked by fallen trees and at one place flooded by a beaver dam, so that it took ten hours to travel as many miles. A straw hat that the British astronomer habitually wore was torn in shreds by the bush. On August 18, in a saddle between snow-capped peaks Anderson found the monument quite intact.

Descending, Captain Anderson met Commissioner Campbell, Major Twining and Lieutenant Green on the way up with pack mules. The first two went only as far as the crest of the Kootenay Pass, but Greene kept on, turning off up the valley of Akamina Brook to the spring from which it flowed to the Flathead and the Columbia

Rivers. Nearby he found a little lake without outlet over-ground and traces of the last astronomical station of the earlier survey, observed by the Americans in 1860 and the British in 1861. In a letter home, August 24, Greene wrote: "Leaving camp this morning, it was a hard scramble up on to the divide and from that with our hands and knees we hauled ourselves up over the rocks, where my dog could not follow, to the top. A quarter of a mile to the Southeast in a saddle of the divide at an altitude of 6,700 feet stands a well shapen pyramid of unhewn limestone . . . It is in an admirable position; from its base you can push a stone loose with your foot and it will go thundering down the mountainside near half a mile into a lake the water of which eventually reaches Hudson's Bay. Looking west you can fire a pistol shot down into another lake which discharges to the Pacific Ocean."

Lieutenant Greene remained at Camp Akamina three days, climbing ridges and triangulating peaks. As others have probably done since, he and the dozen men with him amused themselves carving names on the pyramid and "rolling great bounders down the mountain and watching them with a glass fall into the lakes 40, 50 and even 60 seconds and over from the time we started them." Coming down, they met Mr. Ashe surveying the Kootenay Pass. He had brought the British topographical survey to the St. Mary's River in a three-mile belt and west from there in a six-mile zone to Waterton Lake.

This last area was regarded by the surveyors as a paradise compared to the dried-up plains. They found the soil rich, the grass lush, water and wood abundant, and the north-flowing streams full of fish. Dr. Millman described the St. Mary's as having "plenty of trout in it, beautiful cold and clear water." The Belly River resembled the St.

Mary's, "the water rushing along in rapids over a splendid bed of stones." Here the young doctor spent a day fishing with Captain Featherstonhaugh and "got quite a haul. The heaviest weighed three pounds." Such catches made a welcome supplement to the reduced meat allowance decreed by Captain Cameron. On August 20, Dr. Millman rode over to Waterton Lake with Veterinary Boswell and Carvell the computer, lunched at the American camp with Captain Ames and caught some fine trout at the bottom of a cascade.

The Americans went fishing too, with improvised tackle. Dr. Coues, who found the lake and its tributaries teeming with four varieties of the salmon family, wrote: "The main stem of a stout willow bush, or trunk of a young spruce tree, furnished the rod; any stout cord the line; grasshoppers the bait. The men who were the most successful in taking large salmon used a hook that would do for halibut, extemporized out of the iron handle of an army mess-kettle and baited with a chunk of salt pork." The weight of the fish ran from five to twenty-two pounds, and length twenty-four to forty inches. While his campmates fished for the pot, Dr. Coues observed broods of harlequin duck, as well as Bohemian waxwing. The last he considered "the most interesting single result of the Commission, as far as ornithology is concerned, since it shows that the waxwing breeds on or very near the boundary of the United States."

At the end of August the camps on Waterton Lake were struck for the homeward march. Except for Greene's party, soon to follow, the Americans left for the Sweet Grass Hills on the twenty-seventh. The British astronomical parties pulled up stakes the same day, reaching the depot at St. Mary's crossing, where, Dr. Millman noted, many of the men bought Indian ponies from the whiskey traders at $15 to $50 apiece. Having left the boundary mounds to the last, the parties alternated building them at three-mile intervals, usually camping together at night. According to Dr. Millman, "these mounds are made of stone. They are conical, ten feet in diameter at base and six feet high. They also put a small iron plate in a hole two feet deep and ten feet east of centre of mound. The plate is eight inches in diameter, shaped like a soup plate. It has around the edge 'British and United States Boundary Line.' In the centre is 'North 49th Latitude.'"

Captain Anderson with the survey and reconnaissance parties left the lake, August 29, gathering up the depot-keepers and men as he went along. He had not encountered any Blackfeet, although a few were reported peeping over a hilltop at his camp. "I should like to see something of them," he wrote, "for they are said to be the gentlemen of the plains, and are really well off. We heard that an Indian scout who had appeared at one of our camps had gone back to his camp with the alarming account that we were so numerous that the plain was perfectly *black* with *white* men." At the West Butte depot Anderson picked up subastronomer Burpee and a guard of seven sappers sent back earlier to reinforce the two depot-keepers. While the keepers had been alone, a party of two hundred Piegans had come to call and helped themselves to supplies. The same Indians visited the nearby American depot but were discouraged by the guard of twenty-five soldiers.

Another raid took place at the British subdepot on the East Fork of the Milk River, where likewise there were only two men on guard. Lieutenant Greene learned of it when he reached West Butte, September 2, to find "quite a small city of tents, all our own and the English parties being there and three companies of our escort." (The cavalry and two companies of infantry had departed for Fort Buford in mid-August). As Greene heard the story of the raid, "one day a chief of a band of Yanktons (Sioux) and his son came to call, and catching sight of a fine piece of bacon, remarked that he would take that. The two Englishmen took the chief and his son by the nape of the neck and put them out. Next day they returned with their band of about 100 men, tied up the two Englishmen, divided the supplies at the depot into two parts, took one part and went off! So much for Captain Cameron's opinion that the English flag and red ribbons in their hats would be a sufficient escort."

Greene's comment no doubt reflected the American viewpoint that in Indian country army escorts were indispensable. The British rather prided themselves on not having any, and did not acknowledge any molestation by Indians in their subsequent reports, official or otherwise. But a personal letter of Anderson's confirmed the tale heard by Greene: "The Sioux, a most imprudent tribe, suddenly appeared at one of our depot camps and insisted upon getting half of the food that was stored there. Among other vagaries they broke open a box of candles, lit 26 of them and danced all night for the edification of the unfortunate depot keeper."

Major Twining summed up the Indian situation in a statement quoted in the annual report for 1875 of the Smithsonian Institution, where the collections made by Dr. Coues were eventually deposited: "Northwestern Montana is still the range of immense herds of buffaloes whose numbers, contrary to the commonly received opinion, are constantly increasing. This region is the country of the Blackfoot and Piegan tribes of Indians. It is also the debatable ground of the North Assiniboines, the Gros Ventres of the Prairie and the River Crows; while an occasional war party of Sioux may be found as far northwest as the Sweet Grass Hills. With the exception of the Sioux, these tribes appear to be peaceably enough disposed."

As to the buffaloes increasing, the Smithsonian did not agree, nor did Dawson the geologist. His report quite accurately predicted the extinction of the whole northern herd within a dozen years. He likewise foresaw the development of Montana as a cow country, having observed a band of cattle south of Woody Mountain which had strayed from one of the American army posts. "They were quite wild, and almost as difficult of approach as the buffalo; and notwithstanding the fact that they had come originally from Texas, and were unaccustomed to frost and snow, they had passed through the winter, and were in capital condition."

XIII

RETREAT AND DISPERSAL

FROM the West Butte of the Sweet Grass Hills the British surveyors set out for Woody Mountain and the Americans for Fort Benton. Lieutenant Greene was detailed to trace a meridian line south to Fort Shaw on the Sun River, making the trip in five days with Dr. McGillycuddy, Orrin S. Wilson and thirty men. The party passed near the spot where Major Baker of the 2nd Cavalry had obliterated a Piegan village in the winter of 1870; crossing the Marias River in the vicinity of the Whoop-Up Trail, the surveyors were watched and followed by Indians but not molested. Dr. McGillycuddy's diary notes: "Riplinger's old fort is on Marias, burned down. Piegans buried in trees." Mr. Doolittle meanwhile led the rest of the topographers from the North Branch of the Milk River to Fort Shaw by the Riplinger Road, a traders' track skirting the foothills of the Rockies and passing through the Blackfoot agency.

Major Twining had planned to bring his men back to Bismarck via the Missouri River by Mackinaw boats, of which a number were built to his order at Fort Benton during the summer. These open craft, thirty-five feet long by ten feet in the beam and drawing ten inches of water, were propelled by oars and also carried a square sail. All the parties assembled at Fort Benton by September 11, when Greene arrived from Fort Shaw. Next day the company, except Mr. Campbell and Lieutenant Ladley, who returned overland, embarked in six boats appropriately named for Generals Sheridan, Sherman, Terry and Humphreys, Commissioner Campbell and Major Twining. The *U.S. Grant* was left behind when thirty of the hired men decided to stay in Montana. Dr. McGillycuddy's initial entry of the cruise read: "Made twenty-six miles and camped at mouth of Marias River, where we were joined by artist [William] Cary. We also took a murderer with us." The voyage downstream of twelve hundred miles in eighteen days is fully described by Lieutenant Greene in a letter quoted in the Appendix, except that he fails to mention the murderer. Dr. McGillycuddy supplied these particulars for September 25 and 26: "The prisoner, a condemned murderer from Stillwater, Wis. [*sic*], named Joe Sykes, escaped in the evening with shackles on him . . . Prisoner was recaptured and brought into camp at 8 P.M." From Bismarck, where the surveyors docked on September 30, a special train took them through to St. Paul.

At West Butte a report from Ottawa reached the British that the Cree Indians intended to attack them on the homeward march, somewhere between Woody Mountain and Wood End. This intelligence, first brought by Captain Cameron and later repeated by telegram via Fort

Benton, could not have been fully credited, since the surveyors had passed nowhere through Cree country. Yet as a precaution a rendezvous of all the parties was planned at the Woody Mountain depot, whence the assembled company, 167 strong, would travel together. Dr. Millman, returning with Captain Featherstonhaugh's party of mound builders, saw a great many buffalo on both sides of the Milk River. The doctor's diary entry of September 4, two days after leaving West Butte, read: "Buffalo today were thick as bees. The prairie was black with them. I believe you could see about half a million at once. A large herd came rushing over a hill and almost went through our train. The men opened fire and killed several. For fear they might make a rush on us during the night and stampede the horses, we corralled the wagons, put the tents close together and kept the horses inside. The howling of the wolves at night was almost deafening."

But beyond Milk River Lake, where the Métis and the Assiniboines again were found encamped, the buffalo were no longer seen. The horses suffered from drinking alkaline water, but the men took it sparingly and "only in the shape of tea infusion," according to Captain Anderson. Water carts filled from pools of rain water supplied the march for several days across the arid plain where nothing but cactus grew.

Approaching Woody Mountain, from which the assembled parties started eastward, September 20, Featherstonhaugh and Millman went gunning for prairie chickens. In the Coteau they shot goose and duck which were very numerous on the swamps. This year the equinoctial storm did not strike, nor were prairie fires reported. But on September 24, still west of Wood End, the alarms and rumors from Ottawa bore fruit in an Indian scare. A little after dusk Veterinary Boswell reported that he saw a light some distance off which, he insisted, moved about as though an Indian were signaling. "Owing to this report," wrote Dr. Millman, "watchmen were doubled, every one was ordered to have his rifle at his bedside, and seven rounds of ammunition were issued to each man." Nothing further disturbed the camp but the next evening the same light appeared. "It turned out to be the *setting of Venus.*"

At Turtle Mountain Captain Featherstonhaugh and a small crew left the main party to insert iron plates in the mounds through the cutting. He reached the depot, October 6, to find a few Sioux camped about but everything peaceful. Hay cut and stacked along the return route at twenty-mile intervals furnished abundant forage. The main body arrived back at Dufferin on October 11, five days after the ox-teams, completing a march of 860 miles by road in forty-three days from the Rocky Mountains.

Since the spring a new settlement called Emerson had arisen across the river from Dufferin, with five hundred inhabitants that had come from Wisconsin. A colony of Mennonites from Odessa took up land on the prairie toward Pembina Mountain. Contingents of the new force of Northwest Mounted Police were also in evidence, the first setting out from Dufferin in July to follow the boundary road westward. The police took a new track to the northwest at Wood End, and at the Woody Mountain depot in August Assistant Commissioner Macleod purchased 60,000 lbs. of surplus oats from Commissary Herchmer. A detachment visited the West Butte depot, after the surveyors had abandoned it. Dr. Millman noted, November 29: "Another batch of mounted police arrived under command of Mr. Dickens, son of the famous novel-ist. I spent the evening talking with him."

Dispersal of the British Commission followed at once upon the return to Dufferin. Only a few survey chores remained to be done. Crompton was sent to replace the British mounds with iron pillars, on the line from Red River to the western limit of Manitoba, while Burpee performed the same task eastward along the parallel to Point d'Orme. D'Arcy East planted six pillars along the due south line and built a stone monument where the parallel met the western shore of the Lake of the Woods. In the winter when the swamps were frozen he would erect iron pillars where possible from Point d'Orme to the lake shore. Lieutenant Rowe left for England, Oc-tober 17, and a week later Captain Featherstonhaugh started with most of the sappers for Halifax. Later he would return to Ottawa, where Galwey had already gone to rent a house for the winter.

Captain Anderson was the next to leave, having, as he wrote home, avoided a "collision with Captain Cameron, tho' storms rage around me." One of these concerned a very trivial matter, the marmalade and ale allowance in the officers' mess at Dufferin. Captain Cameron, on scru-tinizing the accounts, charged back to the Royal Engi-neers officers shares of the bill for these items, amounting to about $20 each. He also insisted that they pay £17.14.10 for saddlery, horses and tents supplied them, which he felt should come out of their original £100 allowance for outfit. Anderson, having had enough of rows, acquiesced, but Featherstonhaugh and Galwey vigorously protested the last charge, Featherstonhaugh even going so far as to dispute the debit for marmalade on the grounds that "Her Majesty's Government undertook to furnish the table." Cameron had perforce to refer the appeals to Lord Derby at the Foreign Office, who consulted the War Office, who finally overruled the protests. But Cameron was hoist with his own petard, economically speaking, when later the Foreign Office disallowed his wife's traveling expenses to London and reduced his rental allowance there from £5 to £2.2 a week.

Captain Cameron and the secretary meanwhile busied themselves selling off the remaining stores and livestock of the Commission, with the Northwest Mounted Police becoming the principal purchasers. They bought forty teams of horses and sixty yoke of oxen. Boswell took forty-three horses back to Toronto and even the library was sold. When Captain Ward departed on November 15 with Dr. Burgess and Messrs. King, Ashe and Coster, just as the river froze over, Dr. Millman became the only occupant of the officers' quarters, remaining at Dufferin until after Christmas. Captain Cameron's family had returned so he occupied his own house all winter.

The four Royal Engineers officers and one civilian surveyor foregathered in Ottawa to complete the map work and write reports, while living together in the house Galwey had rented. Six of the Royal Engineers enlisted men accompanied them as clerks and draughtsmen. Captain Anderson passed through Chicago and "saw the remains of the two big fires that the people there are so proud of, the ruins of the second fire of last summer being still very fresh and covering about 60 acres." Arriving at Ottawa, he was summoned at once to dine at Rideau Hall with Lord and Lady Dufferin. Later he was entertained by the new Premier, Alexander Mackenzie, and met some of the Dominion politicians, including Sir John MacDonald. Anderson found himself "delighted with the city of Ottawa. The parliament buildings are very fine, built of a white and pink stone. The Ottawa River which is quite a torrent in places flows thro' the city & the trade in logs and sawn planks is enormous."

Ward and Galwey preferred to stay at home in the evenings playing whist, but Featherstonhaugh enjoyed going out and took a small part in private theatricals at Government House, playing in a skit called "Wooing a Wife." In January Anderson visited Washington to confer with Major Twining, and while there dined with Sir Edward Thornton, the British Minister. By coincidence the dinner was a farewell affair for a Mr. Charlton of the British Legation who had married the daughter of Commissioner Campbell and was taking her back to England.

Two comments by Anderson and Galwey on what to them seemed novel customs in Ottawa are characteristic of the observers. Anderson wrote to his sister: "I think you would find it a good thing to wear what the ladies call a 'cloud' here. It is a long woolen comforter, which goes round and round the neck and round the head and then a yard or two to spare. Lady Dufferin who drives about in an open sleigh on the coldest days is generally completely enveloped in one of these . . . It is ridiculous to see how the gentlemen muffle themselves up in fur coats, principally to show them off, I suppose, though they are indispensable when driving in an open sleigh. I have not been able to discover what amusement there is in driving about in an open sleigh for I always wish to get out and run alongside." Galwey wrote his mother: "I have taken to a new amusement, by name tobogganing, from which I returned black and blue on the first trial. It consists in sliding down the steepest and most precipitous slope one can find on a flat sled. I find that

my sled and I fall out and part company on the way down
. . . It is a most favorite amusement at Government
House. Ladies go in for it. I think they like rolling over
and over with the gentlemen."

While the survey officers were enjoying a relaxed winter in Ottawa after their strenuous activities in the field,
questions concerning the Northwest Angle re-engaged
the attention of the diplomats. Captain Cameron had not
mentioned the subject of the "loop" to the American
Commissioner at their last meeting because instructions
in regard to it did not arrive in time. But when the Foreign Office came to consider a readjustment of the boundary in regard to the entire Northwest Angle, elimination
of the "loop" became part of the larger question. In July,
1874, the Dominion Privy Council precipitated the issue
by urging the desirability of having the boundary follow
the south shore of the Lake of the Woods to its intersection with the 49th parallel. Its thesis was that the anomalous area of the Northwest Angle, intrinsically of slight
value to either country, would become a haven for fugi-
tives and smugglers. After consultation with the Colonial
Office, Lord Derby determined to ask the Canadian Government what consideration it was prepared to offer for
the readjustment, before broaching the subject in Washington. The answer came back: $25,000.

Lord Derby, not very sanguine about offering this sum,
instructed Sir Edward Thornton to sound out the attitude of the United States Government and to suggest a
cession to Canada "on the ground of international convenience, without any payment." The British Minister
was also informed of the intersection of the meandering
channel line with its continuation in the due south line,
in the hope that he could at least get rid of the "loop."

The proposal, originally formulated by Major Wilson, was that the most southerly point of intersection, marked point "B" on a map forwarded to Thornton, be recognized as the northwest point. This would leave the due south line intact but eliminate one-tenth of a square mile of water area, where national jurisdiction would be doubtful in any case.

Sir Edward Thornton sensed a diplomatic advantage in raising the lesser matter first. But his dispatch of February 8, 1875, to Lord Derby reported that on his explaining point "B" to the Secretary of State, "Mr. Fish showed great disinclination to any change of the northwest point . . . marked and considered to be the real point for so many years." When Thornton broached the cession of the Northwest Angle, "Mr. Fish evinced even more disinclination." He said Congress would never agree unless Her Majesty's Government "were prepared to make very great sacrifices." He remarked that the land was important to Canada for a landing on the lake. The British Minister returned to the subject a week later, after there had been a cabinet meeting, but Mr. Fish adhered to his view of inexpediency on point "B" and said a cession of even the smallest territory would not pass Congress. He felt it was better not even to discuss a money consideration.

Secretary Fish's diary entry on these conversations lumps them all into one meeting on February 4, giving a slightly different version: "Sir Edward Thornton wishes, in an informal and unofficial way, to ask a question; which is, as he states it, whether this government would be willing to cede to Great Britain 'a very small portion of territory,' to which I reply that I doubt whether it would be worth while to proceed further with the ques-

tion. He, however exhibits a map [showing point "B"]
. . . I ask the object of the proposed change. He states
for convenience, inasmuch as the boundary now com-
mences wholly in British Territory. I reply that . . .
I see no inconvenience resulting therefrom. He inquires
whether I suppose the United States would have a right
to go into this territory and take observations . . . I
claim that they certainly have, both by treaty and on
general principles . . .

"The second proposition which he wishes informally
to suggest is whether we would entertain a proposition
to change the boundary . . . with a view to give to Great
Britain the projecting piece of land lying south of the
present boundary line and east of the due south line . . .
This piece of land contains as he says about 130 square
miles and is as he says of little value. I call his attention
to the fact that it was on this piece of ground that the
wagon road from Fort Garry has been built and that the
landing . . . is also on this ground (in point of fact this
is what they are after as they have no other convenient
approach to the Lake for communication with Manitoba).

"I tell him that I do not think it worth while to make
the proposal as I do not consider that it would be under
any circumstances entertained. But I then add (jocosely)
that if they will accompany the proposition with an offer
to exchange New Brunswick, Nova Scotia and the Islands
together with the Territory south of the St. Lawrence,
we might possibly consider it . . ."

The British Minister had put the questions and transmitted the answers in diplomatic language. Lord Derby
acknowledged the dispatches, March 1, with the comment
that he never expected Mr. Fish to agree to altering the
boundary line: "It is a subject upon which the Americans

are very touchy. He would be sure to be attacked about it in the press and as it could only have been done by a treaty [he] would have had to consult the Senate." The Northwest Angle, isolated like Point Roberts, would remain part of the United States and constitute its most northern point until the admission of Alaska as a state.

XIV

REPORTS AND MEDALS

FOLLOWING their agreeable winter in Ottawa, three of the Royal Engineers officers returned to England in June, 1875, preceded in April by Captain Ward and Quartermaster Sergeant Armstrong to settle the Commission's accounts at the War Office. Lieutenant Galwey was relieved from duty with the Commission on arrival, and Captain Featherstonhaugh the following December. Cameron, now promoted to major, remained at Dufferin until the summer to complete its liquidation as a base. At an appraised value he sold the buildings to the Dominion Government for an immigration station. The Commissioner had long since reported completion of the British share of the survey and from Winnipeg, on October 4, 1875, he reported that the Americans were about to finish their part. This consisted in Captain Gregory's placing iron pillars at two-mile intervals along the boundary south of Manitoba, east and west of Red River, alternately to those placed by the British the fall and winter before. The pillars were hollow castings in the form of a truncated pyramid, eight feet high and from eight to four inches square. Their opposite faces bore the inscriptions in raised letters, "Convention of London" and "October 20, 1818." Gregory did not reach Pembina to start the work until the beginning of September; in a month he set seventeen pillars east and forty-three west of Red River.

Lieutenant Greene also spent the summer of 1875 in the field, although his work did not directly concern the British. In July, by way of the Union Pacific Railroad to Ogden and stage from there, he journeyed to Montana to complete his meridian line observations and thus establish the exact longitude of the astronomical stations in the vicinity of the Sweet Grass Hills. Men and transportation were furnished him from the military post at Fort Shaw.

As a result of Captain Anderson's trip to Washington, it was arranged that the Americans would come to England for the final closing, to take place in the spring of 1876. Meanwhile Major Cameron arrived with his wife and family in London in November, 1875, and set about preparing his final report. This, with over thirty appendices annexed, was not a skillfully written document. On receipt at the Foreign Office it was characterized as "very bulky and scarcely readable in its present form." Nevertheless, it and its detailed appendices have proved invaluable for a study of the survey.

The British Commissioner's report, dated February 8 but received May 29, 1876, was printed without its annexes for the use of the Foreign Office. It bore the stamp "confidential," which still appears on it. The limited attention that it received may be ascribed, apart from its own content, to the fact that two unofficial but very readable accounts of the survey by Anderson and Featherstonhaugh had already appeared in print. Publication of both these papers was sanctioned by Lord Derby in March and April. Captain Anderson read his, entitled "The North-American Boundary from the Lake of the Woods to the Rocky Mountains," to the Royal Geographical Society on March 27, and Captain Featherstonhaugh's article, "Narrative of the Operations of the British North American Boundary Commission, 1872-76," was printed as a professional paper of the Corps of Royal Engineers. Each was accompanied by a good map, Featherstonhaugh's paper being, if anything, the more lucid.

Another reason why Major Cameron's report may have been restricted in circulation derives from the nature of one of its appendices—a lengthy essay by him "upon the past, present, and future of the North West Canadian Indians." His remarks contained various strictures, perhaps unintended by the author, on the Hudson's Bay Company and on the Dominion Government's policy, since taking over Rupert's Land, in regard to Indian treaties and annuities. Invidious comments were also made respecting missionary efforts and the Indian policy of the United States. Thus, the essay commenced with the statement that "until within the last five years the government of the country, vested in the Honorable Hudson's Bay Company, was entirely subordinated to commercial considerations . . . The Company were essentially fur traders, and the motives which guided their conduct tended directly to encourage the wandering tribes on the great prairies, and the more fixed natives of the wooded and lake districts, to continue their miserable struggle for bare existence." After reciting some oppressive policies of the Company, the paper went on to state that the contrast between "constant warfare in the United States Indian country" and the peaceful condition of British Indians was not due to better government on the British side but to the absence of interference or encroachment by whites. Turning his attention to the church, Cameron wrote: "Missionaries have for many long years labored hard and painfully among these people . . . In no single instance did the expeditionary party see a trace of the adoption of Christianity or of social improvement." The author also cited breaches of faith under Canadian treaties with Indians, likely in his opinion to bring about strife as in the United States, and questioned the adequacy to an Indian of five dollars a year as an annuity. "The measure dealt out to them is chiefly regulated by consideration of the terms upon which peaceful possession of their country may be obtained; and little more is done to assist them in passing from barbarism to civilization than was done by Cæsar for the Britons."

Major Cameron's remedy for all this was education of the Indian children, in institutions placed "within easy reach of the parents' hunting grounds," they to have free access and the children kind treatment. This would lessen if not entirely remove "such dislike as the parents might have to transfer their children from their tents." Stock raising, dairies, poultry keeping, farm produce, rearing and training horses, hut building, brick making, pottery, carpentry, other trades and female domestic work would afford "useful instruction to the pupils." Special religious teaching it would be safer to delay, until the system became well established. Discounting the usual frontier opinion of Indians, Cameron wrote that "on the frontier, the settlers, considering the stock whence they spring, are comparatively much lower in the scale than the Redman whose reduced condition is contemptible even in the eyes of his own kinsmen who still roam in wild freedom." The humanity or practicality of his panacea aside, the document was certainly an irrelevant and tactless one to find attached to the official report of an international boundary commissioner.

In March the two Commissioners exchanged notifications of readiness to close and late in April Commissioner Campbell and Major Twining arrived in London. After a comparison of records and maps by the two chief astronomers, the final meeting was held on May 29, 1876. Present were the two Americans and three Britishers, Major Cameron, Captain Anderson and Captain Ward. The protocol of the meeting noted that the chief astronomers submitted in duplicate a list by name of forty astronomical stations from the Lake of the Woods to the Rocky Mountains, plus one observed at the Northwest Angle; a descriptive list of 388 monuments and marks placed on the boundary, including seven on the due south line; and a set of twenty-four topographical maps, scale one inch to two miles, showing the monuments and marks. There were listed 135 iron pillars, 129 stone cairns, 113 earth mounds, 3 stone and earth mounds, and 8 timber marks (in Roseau Swamp). The northwest point itself, being in water, was not marked, nor was the reference monument rebuilt at the Indians' site listed. These documents were authenticated by the signatures of the Commissioners, who agreed in writing that the monuments "are on and mark the astronomical lines" stipulated by the Treaty of 1818 to be the boundary. In the intervals between monuments along the parallel, they agreed that the line "has the curvature of a parallel of 49° north latitude." Finally they agreed that if any of the monuments were obliterated, the site should be recovered by its recorded position relative to the next unobliterated mark or marks.

From 1872 to 1876 Commissioner Campbell expended $309,007.64 on the survey, his final report showing an unexpended balance of $15,000 from the last Congressional appropriation of $150,000. By subsequent legislation this balance was applied to the publication of an elaborate report of the American Commission. The precise British expenditure is not known, though it is safe to say that it exceeded the 1871 estimate of £100,000. Budgets at Dufferin ran about £50,000 a year and a marginal note in the Foreign Office records, under date of August 26, 1876, gave a total outlay of £157,000 over four years. Perhaps some of this was offset by the sale of surplus supplies. Of course one half of the total was borne by the Dominion Government. The cost was one subject that Major Cameron's report nowhere mentioned.

Included in the extras allowed by the Foreign Office was a charge of £168 from the Tower of London for replacing or repairing the firearms issued to the Royal Engineers. Forty-nine of the fifty-two Adams revolvers taken to Canada in 1872 were returned to store but only twenty-three out of forty-four Snider rifles. Because of the exigencies of frontier service no officer or man was held liable for the loss. Written off, too, was $40 for bank notes missing from a package of $15,000 which Mr. Coster picked up at Winnipeg one frosty morning without counting. Another item was a gratuity of $450 granted to

George Poulter, a wagonmaster whose foot was stepped on by a horse. The Foreign Office reluctantly agreed to severance pay of $1,089.20, allowed by the Dominion Government to four civilians discharged by the Commissioner in 1872. They had been hired in Ontario as clerks or assistants and at Dufferin refused to sign a blanket agreement to perform any sort of work given them.

Likewise paid was a bill of $1,628.15 for printing in Montreal a thousand copies of George Mercer Dawson's 387-page *Report on the Geology and Resources of the Region in the Vicinity of the 49th Parallel from the Lake of the Woods to the Rocky Mountains,* with lists of plants and animals collected and notes on the fossils. In this geological study Dr. Dawson supplied no narrative of his part in the survey, leaving to a separate report his exploration, in August, 1873, of the canoe route from the Lake of the Woods to Red River by way of side streams. This connection had long been known and used by the Chippewa and the Sioux. With two other men in an eighteen-foot canoe, Dawson accomplished the journey of about 160 miles in nine days. From the lake they ascended the short Reed River, portaged seven miles across swamp and muskeg to the headwaters of the East Roseau, and followed that stream down. Beyond Lake Roseau the route entered the West Roseau River, passing for fifty miles through Minnesota. Log jams in the headwaters of the East Roseau made traveling difficult and below Point d'Orme where the West Roseau re-entered Canada the canoe had to be carried around some bad rapids. The exploration was undertaken to find a possible course for a canal to Manitoba, but passage of the route through the United States precluded its utility.

As respects the collections made by Dr. Dawson, who

received enthusiastic help from Drs. Burgess and Millman in the botanical field, and from Sapper Duckworth as a taxidermist, the geological specimens remained in Canada for transmission to its Geological Survey. Zoological specimens of nineteen mammals and 328 birds went to the British Museum and the botanical collection to the Royal Gardens at Kew. The School of Military Engineering at Chatham received 250 photographic negatives. Finally, the astronomical records were deposited at the Royal Observatory in Greenwich.

With the signing of the papers there remained only one bit of unfinished business—the tossing of bouquets. In the United States of those days there were no medals to bestow, and Commissioner Campbell's report showed no partiality in the mention of those who had assisted him. Major Twining, Captain Gregory and Lieutenant Greene were each commended and their reports included with the Commissioner's when it was printed. Major Cameron's views may perhaps be inferred from his report, wherein four lines were devoted to praise of Captain Anderson and twenty-five to Captain Ward. Mr. Boswell, the veterinary, came next with fourteen lines of mention and then Commissary Herchmer with eight. A tribute to the memory of chief scout Hallett was longest of all—forty lines.

But another estimate which undoubtedly carried great weight came to Lord Carnarvon at the Colonial Office in a private letter from the Governor General of Canada. He reported, July 27, 1876, that Dr. Tupper sought to have his son-in-law promoted or given some recognition for his services but that the Premier, Alexander Mackenzie, was reluctant to recommend it because of his political antagonism to Tupper. Commenting on Major Cameron's services, Lord Dufferin wrote: "We have had reason to doubt whether his action as Commissioner did not tend rather to retard and impede than to expedite the work . . . I believe myself, though as an R.E. I must expect my advocacy to be somewhat mistrusted, that the success of this difficult work was due to the science and perseverance of Captain Anderson, the chief astronomer, and the officers and men of R.E. under him, and was achieved in the face of much opposition from the Commissioner: but this is of course only my private opinion." On August 18, Lord Carnarvon acknowledged receipt of a recommendation from the Foreign Office that Captain Anderson be awarded a companionship in the Most Distinguished Order of St. Michael and St. George, otherwise known as the C.M.G. No promise was made but on the same day in May of the following year the Queen graciously bestowed this honor on both the recent Commissioner and the former chief astronomer of Her Majesty's North American Boundary Commission.

XV

SINCE THOSE DAYS

EVEN before the final closing in London there were portents that the boundary marks might not endure permanently. In the fall of 1875, General Selby Smith, Commander-in-Chief of the Canadian Militia, made an inspection tour, visiting some of the newly established posts of the Northwest Mounted Police. Near Waterton Lake he happened to observe some of the boundary cairns built by the surveyors only the year before. His report mentioned that "these, constructed of loose stones, have been nearly demolished by the buffaloes."

But not until thirty-five years later were any official steps taken to preserve or restore the original monuments. As early as 1892 the Province of British Columbia brought to the attention of the Dominion Government the desirability of re-examining and multiplying the marks along its southern border. Five years later, as a result of a study of the Idaho–Montana boundary by the U.S. Geological Survey, it became clear that the unpublished American reports of the 1857-61 survey were lost. The search for the missing papers led, however, to the finding of British counterparts. Eventually new mineral discoveries and overlapping mining claims along the Washington–British Columbia border brought about a joint re-examination of the northwest boundary by Canadian and American engineers, beginning in 1901. Their reports led to the appointment of commissioners to re-monument this boundary, the Canadian representative being William F. King, subassistant astronomer in the 1872-76 survey. For the United States, President Theodore Roosevelt appointed the superintendent of the Coast and Geodetic Survey and the director of the Geological Survey.

As a result of five seasons' work by Canadian and American parties in alternate sectors, all but five of the 161 original marks were recovered and replaced by aluminum-bronze monuments (except the granite obelisk at Point Roberts which still stands.) New monuments were placed at 112 intermediate points surveyed on straight lines between the original marks, and the vistas recut. As a result, the greatest land distance between marks was reduced from 25 miles to 6,210 meters, and in many cases the monuments came within a mile of each other.

This co-operative work resulted in a new treaty adopted, April 11, 1908, between the United States and the United Kingdom, for a re-examination of the entire Canada–United States boundary, Article VII of which ratified the new marks placed west of the Rockies. By Article VI, remonumenting between the Lake of the Woods and the

Rockies was provided for. In the same year, for better enforcement of the customs and immigration laws, President Roosevelt reserved from entry all unpatented public land of the United States within sixty feet of the boundary, and the Province of British Columbia took similar action.

From 1909 to 1913, Canadian and American parties, each accompanied by a representative of the other country, worked along the line east of the Rockies in separate sectors. All but one of the 388 original marks were recovered, the missing cairn being in the town of Portal, North Dakota, about four and a half miles west of the Rivière des Lacs astronomical station. Its site was retrieved by relation to this point and the next one to the west, as provided in the protocol signed May 29, 1876. In locating 653 new intermediate points, mostly along the parallel west of Manitoba where the original monuments were three or more miles apart, the surveyors followed the stipulation of Commissioner Cameron (quoted in the Treaty of 1908) that between the original monuments "the line has the curvature of a parallel of 49° north latitude." This was achieved by surveying straight lines between the old marks, and then calculating offsets to the curve of the parallel. The new points reduced the greatest land interval between marks to 4,955 meters, the average being only a mile and a third. All new points and the sites of old cairns and mounds as far west as the North Branch of the Milk River were marked with cast-iron monuments similar to those placed along the Manitoba border in 1875. From the North Branch to Akamina summit, aluminum-bronze monuments like those placed west of the Rockies were used as markers.

Time and the co-operative spirit engendered by these

Lieut. Galwey's Astronomical Party
Dr. Millman, Dr. Burgess, Lieut. Galwey FRONT ROW LEFT
Pub. Archives Canada

Crow Indians killed by Piegans

Int. Boundary Comm.

General Sheridan and his Staff, Shenandoah Valley, 1864
Maj. Reno FRONT LEFT ARROW
Gen. Sheridan FRONT RIGHT ARROW

New-York Historical Society

United States Boundary Commission
Capt. Gregory, Dr. Coues, Comm'r Campbell,
Maj. Twining, Capt. Bryant SEATED L. TO R.
Bangs, Boss, Lt. Greene, Capt. Ames, Doolittle,
Wilson, Dr. McGillycuddy STANDING

Waterton Lake RIGHT
Int. Boundary Comm.

"Return of the Northern Boundary Survey Party," painted by
William Cary, 1908

Detail by the same Artist, 1874
Dr. Coues LEFT CORNER; Capt. Gregory RIGHT

joint efforts induced the Commissioners, under the Treaty of 1908, to recommend several changes in boundary provisions. The first was a return to the doctrine of straight lines between monuments, as established in 1869 before Commissioner Cameron's predilection for a curve. The change was embodied in Article II of the treaty adopted on February 24, 1925, between the United States and His Britannic Majesty in respect to the Dominion of Canada. This recited that the average distance between adjacent monuments east of the Rockies was now one and one-third miles, and that the deviation of the curve of the 49th parallel from a straight line for this distance was "only one-third of a foot," in no instance exceeding one and eight-tenths feet. It being "impracticable to determine the course of a line having the curvature of a parallel of 49° north latitude on the ground between the adjacent monuments" and yet "desirable that the boundary at any point between adjacent monuments may be conveniently ascertainable on the ground," the parties agreed to define such a line as consisting of "a series of right or straight lines joining adjacent monuments as now established."

The other recommendation, bringing about what Commissioner Cameron had tried but failed to achieve, was a change in the "most northwestern point" to point "B" as indicated on the map sent to Sir Edward Thornton in 1875. Here the recitals of Article I of the same treaty of 1925 referred to the intersection at five points of the line leading to the northwest point with the meridian from it, leaving "two small areas of United States waters in the Lake of the Woods, comprising a total area of two and one-half acres, entirely surrounded by Canadian waters." The contracting parties agreed that the most southerly point of intersection, being latitude 49° 23' 04."49 north and longitude 95° 09' 11."61 west, should be the terminus. After fifty years the United States had relinquished something under a mile of latitude, without even a murmur in the Senate.

One other stipulation in the Treaty of 1925 requires mention. It provided for continuous maintenance of the boundary between Canada and the United States (including Alaska) by permanent Commissioners. They were jointly empowered and directed to inspect the line from time to time, to repair all damaged monuments, to keep boundary vistas open and in the future "to determine the location of any point of the boundary line which may become necessary in the settlement of any question that may arise between the two Governments." The Commissioners were required to submit to their respective governments, at least once a year, a "joint report," and in case of a vacancy among them by death, resignation or disability, "the Party on whose side the vacancy occurs shall appoint an Expert Geographer or Surveyor as Commissioner."

Whether the last two provisions were designed to obviate difficulties that had arisen in the past is hard to say; but it can be stated with confidence that since 1925 and in fact since 1902 there has been steady co-operation between boundary representatives north and south of the border. Although provided for in the Treaty of 1908, there has never been occasion since for reference of a dispute between them to their respective governments for settlement. Over the course of sixty years Canada has had eight Commissioners: William F. King (1902-16), J.J. McArthur (1917-24), J.D. Craig (1925-31), Noel J. Ogilvie (1931-47), James M. Wardle (1947-50), J. Leslie Rannie (1950-51), J.E.R. Ross (1951-57) and A. Frederick Lambert, since 1957. United States Commissioners in the number of nine have been: Charles D. Walcott (1903-08), O.H. Tittmann (1903-15), E.C. Barnard (1915-21), E. Lester Jones (1921-29), James H. Van Wagenen (1929-35), Thomas Riggs (1935-45), John A. Ulinski (1945-53), Samuel L. Golan (1953-61) and Edward J. King since 1961.

Canadian Commissioners are appointed for indefinite terms, their opposite numbers "during the pleasure of the President." Meetings take place every spring, alternating between Ottawa and Washington, and in the summer the Commissioners make a joint inspection trip. Collateral issues beyond the jurisdiction of these Commissioners have been dealt with under the Boundary Waters Treaty of January 11, 1909. A separate International Joint Commission of six members has allocated the use of the St. Mary's and Milk Rivers for irrigation and power, established a suitable water level for the Lake of the Woods, reported on the potentialities of the Souris River and, most recently, on the development of the upper Columbia River for power and flood control.

Experience has shown that the entire line, measuring over 5,500 miles (including the Alaska and water boundaries) must be gone over at least once in ten years to repair or replace monuments or buoys. Vistas amounting to 1,353 miles require periodic clearing. In 1928 the vistas were recut from the Red River to the Northwest Angle and in 1932 through Pembina and Turtle Mountains. From 1930 to 1936 all vistas west of the Rockies were cleared. This work has been repeated several times since, the latest clearings being Red River to the Northwest Angle, 1957; Pembina Mountain, 1956; Turtle

Mountain, 1953; and east and west of the Rockies 1955-60. From 1925 to 1937 fifty-one additional intermediate marks were established at road crossings, surveyed on straight lines between existing monuments. Since then thirty-eight marks have been added at various points and forty-two repaired, replaced or replumbed. Most of the new monuments are concrete obelisks, marked "International Boundary" on the side facing the highway and "Treaty of 1925" opposite. "Canada" and "United States" appear on the north and south faces.

By treaty each government is required to pay its own Commissioner and staff, while jointly incurred expenses in maintaining the boundary are to be divided. The annual appropriation for the United States section of what is presently called the International Boundary Commission, United States and Canada, approximates $100,000.

As a result of the re-examination of the boundary and other detailed surveys, a geodetic 49th parallel has been established which is sometimes north and sometimes south of the agreed line shown on International Boundary Commission maps. At only one monument in a thousand (No. 490, in Montana) do the two lines coincide at the exact latitude of 49° 00′ 00″ 00, in accordance with the original definition of the Astronomer Royal. In the latitude of the parallel a second of measurement represents about a hundred feet of distance. Co-ordinates for the monuments as published by the Commission show an extreme variance of 11.96 seconds from the norm. At some two hundred marks the difference amounts to over four seconds (400 feet) and for eight hundred, at least one second (100 feet).

The geodetic parallel is not precisely the same as the mean calculated in Major Twining's report of 1876 or that laid down in 1861 between the Similkameen and Kettle Rivers. At the latter point the agreed boundary still runs about 75 feet north. From Point Roberts to Sumas it runs 800 or 900 feet north and at the Belly River and West Butte 900 and 1200 feet south. Thus the extreme disparities are greater even than those computed at the time of the initial survey.

At the Lake of the Woods the northwest point, as redefined, is still in water and still unmarked. But cast-iron reference monuments stand at the given latitude on each side of it within about 1,500 feet. The Northwest Angle has become a Minnesota State forest; apart from vacationists its population numbers under one hundred persons. In summer the area can only be reached from the outside by boat or plane, although in wintertime the due south cutting still serves as an access road to haul pulp and timber. Immediately west of this line the Province of Manitoba has established the Northwest Angle Forest Reserve.

At Turtle Mountain, once frequented by a few renegade Sioux, an Indian reservation south of the line presently accommodates about sixty-five hundred Chippewa and mixed bloods. The International Peace Garden, consisting of several thousand landscaped acres donated by the State of North Dakota and the Province of Manitoba, straddles the boundary about fifteen miles east of Lake Farquhar, now called Lake Metigoshe. Here a state park with eight hundred summer cottages has replaced the dense growth of trees reported by Lieutenant Greene. Just north of the line lies Manitoba's Turtle Mountain Forest Reserve.

At the first crossing of the Souris, a U.S. national wildlife refuge extends southward along the river for fifty miles. Similar Federal sanctuaries for ducks have been established below the second crossing of this river and along the neighboring Rivière des Lacs. They provide important resting points for migratory birds on the Mississippi Flyway.

The 49th parallel is now straddled by several dozen communities which have grown up next to the boundary in one country or the other. There are over fifty road crossings with customs and immigration stations on either side of the line. At twenty-five points railroad tracks cross. To eliminate so-called "line houses," the Dominion of Canada has recently enacted a law to preclude the further construction of buildings within ten feet of the international boundary. Legislation to the same effect is contemplated in the United States.

A general highway or railroad map of North America suggests several inferences respecting the 49th parallel line. That it forms an economic barrier is obvious enough, yet no more than any customs division on the continent would. That it presents obstacles to easy travel between points in Canada and the United States is less evident, although diagonal crossings of the parallel are rare, the principal one being in mid-continent from northwest to southeast and the reverse. This route skirts the Coteau of the Missouri, which perhaps accounts for its oblique direction. A major crossing northeast or southwest is not discernible; most routes run directly north or south to connect with preponderant east or west traffic. On the airways this is even more apparent. That the latitudinal boundary bisects rather than separates watersheds has, if anything, equalized the division of their use or of the power which they generate. That the people who have come to live on either side of the line are complacent today about its location speaks well for boundary peace and permanence.

The first beneficiaries of the 49th parallel line were undoubtedly the Sioux under Sitting Bull, who late in the 1870's took refuge north of it. On several occasions Col. Nelson A. Miles of the Yellowstone Command sought to cross over in pursuit, without first obtaining permission from the Canadian authorities. He was restrained by explicit warnings from General Sherman. Several years later the Sioux returned to the United States of their own accord. The reverse of this situation took place almost twenty years later, when the United States wished to deport to Canada some refugee Cree Indians who had come south of the border into Montana after the Riel Rebellion of 1885. But on this occasion there was negotiation between the two Governments first. Then about five hundred Indians were escorted to the boundary by U.S. Army units and received there by members of the Northwest Mounted Police. The lack of border forays or incidents of violence, once the line became definitive, testifies further to its general durability.

Of the men who ran the line in 1872-76 a postscript may well be added. Commissioner Campbell held no further public office and died in Washington in 1887 at the age of seventy-four. Commissioner Cameron appeared once more in a boundary matter as the author of a "Report on the location of the British-Alaskan Boundary under the Anglo-Russian Convention of 1825." This was published by the Colonial Office in 1886. In it Colonel Cameron suggested purchase from the United States of the Alaska panhandle for £50,000 to £100,000. The next year he retired from the army, being gazetted out with the rank of major general. In 1888, at the instance of Sir John Macdonald who ten years earlier had resumed the Premiership of Canada, General Cameron was appointed commandant of the Royal Military College at Kingston, Ontario, a post he held until the Dominion Government changed in 1896. A few years later he returned to his native heath at Dingwall, Scotland, dying there in 1921 at the age of eighty-seven. An obituary in the *Ross-Shire Journal* noted that "those who knew him best were struck with the almost military method and order which ruled the common actions of his daily life. His particularity entered into everything; exactness and precision were his constant care and loose statement of fact, unsupported by evidence, had no place in his conversation."

Neither of the two chief astronomers, men of great promise in their chosen profession, lived more than five or six years after conclusion of the survey and each suffered a coincidental fate. William J. Twining, whose brevet rank of major became substantive in 1877, was appointed as the first engineer member of the Board of District Commissioners at Washington. In this post he served the capital city with distinction for four years, until his sudden death from pneumonia on May 5, 1882. He had caught cold after a day's fishing in the Potomac. To Lieutenant Greene at his bedside his last words were: "I am not afraid. Have me buried at West Point." When he died at the age of forty-two Twining was still a bachelor.

Samuel Anderson married his second cousin, Louisa Dorothea Brown, in August, 1876. He became Assistant Inspector of Submarine Defenses at the War Office, achieving his majority in 1879, the same year in which he served as British Commissioner for the delimitation of the Servian frontier under the Treaty of Berlin. In August, 1881, just after becoming Inspector of Submarine Defenses, he went to Scotland for a month's fishing and took a chill the last day. It turned into fever and he died within a week at about the same age as Twining. Anderson's commanding officer, concluding a tribute to him, wrote: "His character was singularly unselfish."

Of the other engineer officers, Featherstonhaugh, Galwey and Ward continued in routine army careers, becoming respectively commandants of Royal Engineers at Newcastle-on-Tyne, Mauritius and Woolwich, before retirement in the 1890's. The first two reached the rank of colonel, and Ward and Rowe, lieutenant colonel. The last retired in 1884 after teaching surveying at Woolwich and came to Canada as a missionary, but poor health forced his return to England. All but Featherstonhaugh married, Ward's bride being a daughter of the Bishop of Bath.

Captain Gregory served as chief engineer of the Department of the Missouri and aide-de-camp to General Sheridan for five years. He was promoted to major in 1886, married later, and died in 1897. In the army he became known as the author of a *Telegraphic Code to Insure Secrecy,* published in 1885.

Francis Vinton Greene, the youngest of all the engineer officers, enjoyed the most outstanding career. In 1877-78 he served as an American military observer at the Russo-Turkish War, accompanying the invading army at the battles of Shipka, Plevna and Sophia. This experience provided material for a book, *The Russian Army and its Campaigns in Turkey.* In 1886, after a year as professor of military engineering at West Point, Captain Greene resigned from the army to enter business.

Becoming colonel of the 71st Regiment, New York National Guard, in 1892, he was ordered to Cuba in 1898 and later to the Philippines. There he commanded the American forces in the Battle of Malate and was promoted to major general of volunteers. In 1902 during the term of Mayor Seth Low, General Greene served as police commissioner of New York City. Besides a book called *Sketches of Army Life in Russia* he was the author of *The Revolutionary War and the Military Policy of the United States, The Mississippi Campaigns in the Civil War* and a life of his kinsman, General Nathanael Greene.

Among the civilian staff on the survey, many had notable careers. Lewis Boss became director of the Dudley Observatory at Albany and Charles L. Doolittle held the same post in the Flower Observatory at the University of Pennsylvania. William F. King continued in government surveying in Canada, becoming, in 1890, chief astronomer in the Department of the Interior. Before his appointment in 1902, previously mentioned, he served from 1893-95 as British Commissioner on boundary questions between Canada and Alaska and in Passamaquoddy Bay. Dr. Valentine T. McGillycuddy became agent to the Sioux Indians at Pine Ridge Reservation, Dakota Territory, and the subject of a noteworthy biography by his wife. Dr. Thomas Millman returned to the practice of medicine in Toronto, always maintaining his interest in Canadian flora. At his death in 1921, his collection of three thousand specimens was presented to the University of Toronto. Under the title *Impressions of the West in the Early Seventies,* Dr. Millman's remarkable journal of the survey was published in 1928. Commissary Lawrence Herchmer, following an appointment as inspector of Indian agencies, became Commissioner of the Northwest Mounted Police in 1886. He held the post for fifteen years, retiring in 1900 after a brief period as commander of the first contingent of Canadian volunteers in the Boer War.

Two men whose names lent much distinction to the survey, then or later, were the scientific members, Dr. Elliott Coues (1842-99) and Dr. George M. Dawson (1849-1901). In 1876 the former became secretary and naturalist to the United States Geological and Geographical Survey of the Territories. Its bulletin for July 29, 1878, published his "Field Notes on Birds observed in Dakota and Montana along the 49th Parallel during the Seasons of 1873 and 1874." Dr. Coues resigned from the army in 1880 and, perhaps influenced by his own journeys up the Missouri River, devoted himself, apart from scientific pursuits, to editing narratives of western exploration. Besides producing the first annotated edition of the travels of Lewis and Clark (1893), he edited the journals of Zebulon Pike, Jacob Fowler, Alexander Henry and David Thompson. He also published *Forty Years a Fur Trader on the Upper Missouri, The Personal Narrative of Charles Larpenteur, 1833-1872*. Dr. Coues' *Key to North American Birds*, originally appearing in 1872 and rewritten in 1884, was perhaps his best-known ornithological work.

Following his service with the Boundary Commission, Dr. Dawson joined the Geological Survey of Canada, of which he became assistant director in 1883 and director in 1895. In the late eighties he conducted the first geological study of the Yukon Territory, Dawson City being named for him. As an incidental tribute, the red-backed mouse peculiar to the Klondike region received the scientific designation *Evotomys Dawsoni*. In 1888 the Canadian geologist was summoned to Washington to confer with the superintendent of the Coast and Geodetic Survey on the boundaries of Alaska, at a time when the subject was first considered by a joint high commission. Dr. Dawson served on the Bering Sea Commission in 1891-92 and received the C.M.G. in recognition of his work. Numerous monographs by him appeared in scientific journals and in the reports of the Geological Survey, and he was likewise the author of several full-length works on Canadian geology. His 1875 report has become a highly prized and exceedingly rare book.

Significant, too, in support of the boundary survey were the escorts. All the officers and men of Captain Keogh's Company I of the 7th Cavalry perished with General Custer on June 25, 1876, in battle with the Sioux at the Little Big Horn. Captain Weir and most of his Company D survived the battle, being part of the battalion assigned to Captain Benteen. But Weir died later that year. Major Reno also survived the battle, to become the target of much criticism. An official inquiry into his conduct as the ranking officer next to Custer found nothing to censure, but on other grounds he was dismissed from the army in 1880 and died in 1889. Captain Ames of the 6th Infantry resigned his commission in 1876 and died in 1882. Captain Bryant of the same regiment continued in the army to become colonel of the 13th Infantry in 1888 and retire six years later. Captain Harbach, whose company of the 20th Infantry escorted the surveyors in 1872-73, became colonel of the 1st Infantry in 1899, retiring later as a brigadier general.

Two men behind the scenes wind up the roster of participants. Dr. Charles Tupper, the influential father-in-law of Commissioner Cameron, in 1884 became High

Commissioner for Canada in London, Prime Minister of the Dominion in 1896 and died a baronet. Charles W. Wilson, who threw his weight in support of Captain Anderson at the Foreign Office, became a major general of Royal Engineers, K.C.B., K.C.M.G. He was knighted a second time for his part in the Nile Expedition to relieve General Gordon. Originally the chief of intelligence, he succeeded to command of the advance column when Sir Herbert Stewart was mortally wounded at Gubat in January, 1885. Aboard an armored steamer, Wilson came within sight of Khartum a week later, only to learn that the Mahdi had stormed the place the day before and killed Gordon.

The memory of a few of the surveyors of 1872-76 has been preserved in place names along the 49th parallel, in the vicinity of Waterton Lakes National Park. Here we find Cameron Lake and Falls, Rowe Lakes, Anderson Peak, Mt. Galwey and Mt. Boswell, with Mt. Campbell just across the line in Glacier National Park. But the name of Lake Farquhar in Turtle Mountain has disappeared, even on International Boundary Commission maps, and of course Dufferin long ago became West Lynne, Manitoba. Later triangulation stations have been given such distinctive names as Bud, Joe, Gus and Pete, but none has been called after the original surveyors. If further place names are sought, what could be more appropriate and distinctive than Featherstonhaugh or McGillycuddy?

NOTE ON SOURCES

LETTERS

This book has no footnotes because it is written largely from manuscript material—letters, diaries, reports and records that have never been printed. The principal letter sources are the letters of Samuel Anderson to his sister Janet and his mother, recently acquired by the Library of Yale University from a great-nephew. The collection numbers over sixty for the period 1872-75. Another British source is the letters of William J. Galwey to his mother, some seventeen in number, covering the same period. They remain in family possession. For the American side, the best letter collection consists of the letters written by Francis Vinton Greene to his parents in 1873-74. Over thirty are in the Manuscript Division of the New York Public Library, and the last and longest, dated September 13-30, 1874 (reproduced by permission in the Appendix), is part of the Western Americana Collection at Yale. A couple of letters written by Lawrence Herchmer come from the Alexander Campbell Papers in the Provincial Archives of Ontario.

DIARIES

Diaries quoted are four: the manuscript diary of Hamilton Fish, for 1870 and 1875, in the Manuscript Division of the Library of Congress; the diary of Dr. Valentine T. McGillycuddy, for 1874, in the Western Americana Collection at Yale; the diary of James F. Bangs, for 1873, published in State Historical Society of North Dakota, *Collections*, Vol. IV (1913), pp. 219-34; and the journal of Dr. Thomas Millman, for 1873-74, a most informative source, published in Women's Canadian Historical Society of Toronto, *Transactions*, No. 26 (1928). Supplementing these diaries are two official reports by Maj. Marcus A. Reno, 7th Cavalry, relating to the survey escort. These manuscripts are at the National Archives, Civil War Branch (Record Group No. 98), M.D. Mo. 3194 (1873) and 4765 (1874).

FOREIGN OFFICE RECORDS

Official sources are both in manuscript and printed. The Foreign Office records, for 1870-76, in Series F.O. 5/1474-77, 1505-06, 1532, 1666-70, of which the original volumes are in the Public Record Office in London, but available on microfilm at the Public Archives of Canada at Ottawa, contain a wealth of material. They include the "confidential" printed estimate of Colonel Hawkins; the like printed final report of Commissioner Cameron; numerous manuscript annexes to the latter; and correspondence between the Foreign Office and the War and Colonial Offices, the British Minister in Washington, the Governor General of Canada, the Astronomer Royal and Commissioner Cameron. Among the manuscript annexes above noted are annual reports by Captain Anderson, for 1872-74, giving detailed accounts of the progress of the survey. The Public Archives of Canada also have a file of original manuscript reports on various aspects of the work by Captain Featherstonhaugh, Lieutenant Galwey, D'Arcy East, William A. Ashe, William F. King and

A.L. Russell. Printed progress reports by Commissioner Cameron are found in *Sessional Papers, 1875,* Parliament of Great Britain, Vol. 82, p. 53, and *Sessional Papers, 1876,* Parliament of Great Britain, Vol. 82, p. 359.

STATE DEPARTMENT RECORDS

The State Department records, for 1872-76, consist of manuscript material (Record Group No. 76) in the Diplomatic Division, the National Archives, Washington, and an elaborate published report. The manuscripts comprise a file of original letters received, 1872-76, by Commissioner Campbell, with an indexed book abstracting them; bound copies of letters sent, likewise indexed; and a ledger of disbursements, for 1872-76. The first two provide a complete file of correspondence between the American and British Commissioners and between Commissioner Campbell and the Secretary of State. There are also, in manuscript, annual reports of progress by Colonel Farquhar and Major Twining, three work reports by Lieutenant Greene and three significant notebooks containing the day-to-day journal of the topographical party under Lieutenant Greene, for 1873-74. The printed material consists of the final reports of Commissioner Campbell, Major Twining, Captain Gregory and Lieutenant Greene, published in *Reports upon the Survey of the Boundary between the Territory of the United States and the Possessions of Great Britain from the Lake of the Woods to the Summit of the Rocky Mountains, authorized by an Act of Congress approved March 19, 1872* (Government Printing Office, 1878).

This volume is supplemented and brought up to present times by another State Department publication, *Joint Report upon the Survey and Demarcation of the Boundary between the United States and Canada from the Gulf of Georgia to the Northwesternmost Point of the Lake of the Woods* (Government Printing Office, 1937). The latter supplies particulars on the boundary west of the Rockies, which may also be found in Marcus Baker, *Survey of the Northwestern Boundary of the United States 1857-1861,* U.S. Geological Survey, Bulletin No. 174, 1900; Otto Klotz, "The History of the Forty-ninth Parallel Survey West of the Rocky Mountains," *Geographical Review,* Vol. 3 (May, 1917), pp. 382-87; and Col. Charles M. Watson, *The Life of Major-General Sir Charles William Wilson* (London, 1909), pp. 13-40. This survey has recently received attention in Herman J. Deutsch, "A Contemporary Report on the 49° Boundary Survey," *Pacific Northwest Quarterly,* Vol. 53 (January, 1962), p. 17.

OTHER PRINTED MATERIAL

As to printed sources other than the above, details about Major Long's observations at Pembina are given in William H. Keating, *Narrative of an Expedition to the Source of St. Peter's River* (London, 1825), Vol. 2, pp. 38 and 42. The Fenian raid from Pembina is described in Report of the Secretary of War, 1871 (Report of General Hancock, Department of Dakota), 42nd Cong. 2nd Sess., Serial 1503, House Ex. Doc. 1, p. 29; and *St. Paul Pioneer* (November 9-10, 1871). The story of "Lord" Gordon is told in William W. Folwell, *History of Minnesota* Vol. III (St. Paul, 1926), pp. 362-88. Dr. Elliott Coues' observations in Montana and those of Joseph H. Batty are taken from *American Naturalist,* Vol. 9 (September 9, 1874), p. 75; *Forest & Stream,* Vol. 3 (September 24 and October 1, 1874), pp. 99 and 114; *American Sportsman,* Vol. 5 (October 3 and December 26, 1874, and March 6 and 27, 1875), pp. 1, 193, 355, 402; and *Bulletin of the U.S. Geological and Geographical Survey of the Territories,* Vol. IV, No. 3 (July 29, 1878), pp. 545-661. Dr. George M. Dawson's article, "Lignite Formations of the West," appeared in *Canadian Naturalist,* Vol. VII, New Series (April, 1874), p. 241, and his "Notes on the

Locust Invasion of 1874 in Manitoba and the North West Territories," in Vol. VIII, New Series (1876), p. 119.

Gov. Isaac Stevens' report on the North Pacific railroad route, including A.W. Tinkham's descriptions of the Souris and Milk Rivers and the Sweet Grass Hills, is found in *Reports of Explorations and Surveys, to Ascertain the Most Practicable and Economical Route for a Railroad from the Mississippi River to the Pacific Ocean, 33rd Cong. 2nd Sess.,* Serial 791, House Ex. Doc. 91, Vol. 1 (Washington, 1855), pp. 84, 91, 94, 162, 226, 357, 454. Captain Palliser's observations at Pembina in 1857 are described in *Papers relative to the Exploration by Captain Palliser of that portion of British North America which lies between the North Branch of the River Saskatchewan and the Frontier of the United States; and between the Red River and Rocky Mountains* (London, H.M. Stationery Office, 1859) p. 12.

Lord Dufferin's letter of July 27, 1876, is quoted from *Dufferin-Carnarvon Correspondence, 1874-1878,* C.W. De-Kiewiet and F.H. Underhill, eds. (Toronto, The Champlain Society, 1955), p. 248. *The Correspondence of Sir John Macdonald,* Sir John Pope, ed. (New York, 1921), contains a letter, p. 432, from Sir Charles Tupper mentioning General Cameron. There are other references to him in *Begg's Red River Journal and Other Papers,* W.L. Morton, ed. (Toronto, The Champlain Society, 1956), pp. 161, 176, 243; and in Charles C. Tansill, *Canadian-American Relations, 1875-1911* (New Haven, Yale University Press, 1943), pp. 133, 147, 153, where his report on the Alaskan boundary is discussed. Two companion volumes published by the Yale University Press for the Carnegie Foundation, Percy E. Corbett, *The Settlement of Canadian-American Disputes* (1937), p. 17, and Lester B. Shippee, *Canadian-American Relations, 1849-1874* (1939), p. 240, dwell on the San Juan controversy but do not mention the land boundary surveys of 1857-62 and 1872-76.

Details as to Col. Nelson A. Miles on the border are found in Virginia W. Johnson, *The Unregimented General* (Boston, Houghton Mifflin Co., 1962), pp. 211, 214, 217. The deportation of the Crees is described in Report of the Commissioner, Northwest Mounted Police, 1896, Appendix C, and in John E. Parsons, "The Last Indian Removal," *The Westerners Brand Book New York Posse,* Vol. 1, No. 3 (New York, 1954), pp. 6, 9, 19, 22.

MEMOIRS

Memoirs of Maj. William J. Twining were published in U.S. Military Academy Association of Graduates, *Annual Report,* 1882, pp. 94-101, and in U.S. Engineer Bureau, *Professional Memoirs,* Vol. 8 (1916), pp. 504-07. Maj. Samuel Anderson's obituary appeared in *The Royal Engineers Journal* (November 1, 1881), p. 227, and General Cameron's in the *Ross-Shire Journal* (December 30, 1921). For notes on Archibald Campbell and his engineer officers Twining, Gregory and Greene, see Gen. George W. Cullom, *Biographical Register of the Officers and Graduates of the U.S. Military Academy,* Nos. 809, 1998, 2062, and 2312. A memoir of Dr. Elliott Coues appeared in National Academy of Science, *Biographical Memoirs,* Vol. 6 (1909), pp. 397-445, and one of Dr. George M. Dawson in Royal Society of Canada, *Proceedings and Transactions,* Series 2, Vol. 8 (1902), pp. 183-201. Julia B. McGillycuddy wrote the biography of her husband entitled *McGillycuddy, Agent* (Stanford, Stanford University Press, 1941).

PERIODICALS

Two unofficial accounts of the 1872-76 survey have been mentioned in the text: Captain Samuel Anderson, "The North-American Boundary from the Lake of the Woods to the Rocky Mountains," *Royal Geographical Society Journal,* Vol. 46 (London, 1876), p. 228, and Captain Albany Featherstonhaugh, "Narrative of the Operations of the British North American Boundary Commission 1872-76," *Professional Papers of the Corps of Royal Engineers*, Vol. XXIII, New Series (Woolwich, 1876), pp. 24-49. The latter's earlier paper "Notes on the Defenses of Petersburg" appeared in *Professional Papers*, Vol. XIV, New Series (Woolwich, 1865), p. 190.

Several well-illustrated articles on the western boundary surveys between the United States and Canada have appeared in recent periodicals: John Peter Turner, "The Historic Forty-ninth," *Royal Canadian Mounted Police Quarterly*, Vol. 9 (October, 1941 and January, 1942), pp. 167 and 270; Wallace Stegner, "History Comes to the Plains," *American Heritage*, Vol. VIII, No. 4 (June, 1957), pp. 14 and 108; Marjorie Forrester, "Shooting the Stars and Chaining the Land," *The Beaver* (Spring, 1960), p. 10; "That Northwest Angle," *The Beaver* (Autumn, 1960), p. 32. A pictorial story entitled "The Long Border that Peace Built" was published by *Life*, Vol. 49, No. 11 (September 12, 1960), p. 44. The Northwest Angle as it appears today is pictured in: William H. Nicholas, "Men, Moose and Mink of Northwest Angle," *National Geographic*, Vol. XCII, No. 2 (August, 1947), p. 265; and George Silk, "Life at 50 Below," *Life*, Vol. 28, No. 8 (February 20, 1950), p. 101.

MAPS

The twenty-four original maps of the boundary, on a scale of one inch to two miles, signed by the Commissioners in 1876, are in the Foreign Office Library, London, F.O. 5/1566 B. Likewise deposited there and in the Washington office of the International Boundary Commission, United States and Canada, are sets of photozincographed copies. The State Department's *Reports upon the Survey of the Boundary*, etc., published in 1878, contains a printed "Reconnaissance Series" of six sheets, on a scale of one inch to eight miles, showing the boundary and general terrain from the Lake of the Woods to the Rocky Mountains. Ten original sketch maps of the reconnaissances made by Captain Anderson in 1873 and 1874 are contained in Volume F.O. 5/1670 at the Public Record Office, London. One of these maps is reproduced as the back end paper of this book. The front end-paper map comes from Volume M.R. 500/229 in the Public Record Office. For the most recent official maps of the international boundary from the Gulf of Georgia to the Lake of the Woods, see a series of sixty sheets, including index, on a scale of one inch to one mile, published in 1913-27 by the International Boundary Commission, and accompanying its joint report of October 27, 1937.

PHOTOGRAPHS

The photographs taken by the Royal Engineers in 1872-74 and reproduced in this book come from three collections: Dr. Millman's album, which Miss Millman permitted to be copied (credited as Millman); the collection of the American Section, International Boundary Commission (credited as Int. Boundary Comm.); and the collection in the Public Archives of Canada, derived from an album in the Foreign Office Library (credited as Pub. Archives Canada). In these collections many of the same pictures are duplicated. No trace of the original glass plates deposited in 1876 at the School of Military Engineering, Chatham, has been found. They are believed to have been destroyed by bombing in World War II.

APPENDIX

Down the Missouri by Mackinaw Boat

JOURNAL OF LIEUT. FRANCIS VINTON GREENE

September, 1874

On the Missouri River
Sunday Sept. 13th 1874

My Dear Parents:—

I find that wind and water interfere so much with ordinary writing facilities that I have abandoned them, & will occupy myself on the way down with filling part (or all) of this note book with letters.

I am somewhat behind hand with my journal. I believe the last regular letter I wrote was from the Sweet Grass Hills or Three Buttes.

SEPTEMBER 2ND

I arrived there on the 2nd of Sept. and found quite a small city of tents, all our own and the English parties being there & 3 Cos. of our escort. While we had been away, ourselves & the English had each a supply depot there, ours guarded by 25 men & the English by 2 men with red ribbons on their hats, & the English flag flying over the tent!—the two depots were about 1500 feet apart. One morning a party of about 200 Piegan (Blackfeet) Indians came to make a friendly call, and thinking that English hospitality was not quite equal to its world wide reputation, quietly helped themselves to whatever they wanted. They came over to our depot but the Sergt. of the detachment turned out his men and summarily ordered them off. They did not care to fight and left.

We also heard that at another English depot about 100 miles east, also guarded by two men with red ribbons and the English flag, one day a chief of a band of Yanktons (Sioux) & his son came to call, and catching sight of a fine piece of bacon, remarked that he would take that. The two Englishmen took the chief & his son by the nape of the neck & put them out. Next day they returned with their band of about 100 men, tied up the two Englishmen, divided the supplies at the depot into two parts, took one part and went off! So much for Capt. Cameron's opinion that the English flag and red ribbons in their hats would be a sufficient escort.

The Sweet Grass Hills were quite full of the Rocky Mountain sheep. They are about as large as a large deer, of a light dun color and have immense horns shaped like those of a goat. A pair that Lieut. Townsend got were four inches in diameter at the base and 28 inches long. Their hair is in texture almost exactly like that of an antelope and altogether they seem to be a mixture of goat, sheep, deer and antelope. They have a great fondness for running up rocky hills, but are not difficult to kill; by climbing the ridges and then approaching through brush, one can get very close to them, and when disturbed they always run *up* hill. The meat is very good though the mutton taste is not very distinct.

SEPTEMBER 3RD

I separated again on the 3rd of Sept. from the other parties, Twining taking the rest direct to Benton & myself with two parties going towards Fort Shaw. I had already sent one party to that point from the foot of the mountains to reconnoitre the head waters of the various streams flowing towards the Missouri. My object in going to Shaw was to trace a meridian from a known point of our line to the neighborhood of Fort Shaw where there is a telegraph line down to the Union Pacific road. Next summer when it gets too hot for comfort in Washington, I am going up there to observe the longitude by telegraph. The longitude by this method is wonderfully accurate and it will be a check on our longitude by continuous chaining on the parallel from which our maps will be constructed. I expect to make a summer of it taking my time, locating all the posts in Montana and making a trip up into the Yellowstone Park.

SEPTEMBER 8TH

I reached Fort Shaw on the 8th, after passing over a rather forlorn flat alkaline country, crossing the large branches of the Upper Missouri—the Marias and Teton Rivers, and making one dry camp—the only one of the season. It was the third day out; we left the Marias river about 6 o'clock and had to make a long detour to the east to get up the bad lands on to the prairie. I had with me two "water carts"—100 gallon casks mounted on wheels & drawn by a mule—which we have had all summer for just such an emergency. Of course I had them filled. Marching 28 miles over a very flat country without seeing a drop of water, a little before dark I spurred up my tired horse and rode ahead on to a little knoll and searched eagerly with my glass for any signs of surface water or for the banks of the Teton River which I thought could not be far off. I could see neither, so I started back as rapidly as possible to find the train before dark and stop them; dropping behind me a scout on a thoroughly jaded horse, who did not find camp till late in the night. I narrowly missed losing the train, as the sun had set & the stars were not out and there were a lot of hummocks on the prairie just large enough to hide the wagons.

I caught sight of something white however, off to my right and about a mile, & soon caught them, stopped the wagons just where they were and put up a few tents, ordering the two water carts to be backed up in front of my tent & unhitched there. We had just about enough water for cooking and drinking purposes—washing went by the board. The poor mules were turned loose to pick what little grass there was.

It was amusing as well as pitiful to see them come smelling of the water carts—one of them was smart enough, while my back was turned, to turn the spigot with his teeth and catch a good drink from the drip pail.

Next morning we moved out before daylight and after 8 miles march got a good camp on the Teton, where I stayed all day. These dry camps for travelers not provided with water carts or casks are a terrible thing. Night finds them almost parched with thirst from the day's tramp over dusty and often dazzling alkaline plains, tired also, and hungry. Eating only increases the thirst, which is so great as to prevent sleep. I made a camp of this kind last autumn and shall not forget it.

I was without military escort, having 40 of my own men and half armed. We were passing through Blackfeet country, that part of it occupied by the Piegan band; it seems we passed quite close to their camp on the Marias river, for the next day some of them met the men at work on the meridian line. They asked for food of course, but made no demonstrations. Five years ago this was as bad a tribe of Indians as could be found west of the Mississippi. You may perhaps remember that in the spring of 1870 the Peace Commissioners called loudly for the blood & head of Maj. E.M. Baker, the author of the "Atrocious Piegan Massacre." With three Companies of his Reg't—the 2nd Cav'y—this Maj. Baker, one morning before daylight, surprised a large camp of these Piegans in the Marias bottom (about where my trail crossed it) and totally wiped them out—extinguished them forever for this world. A few women and children were brought in prisoners—the rest of the camp were decently buried I think. Perhaps he was a little cruel, but from that day to this no one has ever heard of Piegan depredations,—and for my part I owe my cordial thanks to Maj. Baker for being able to travel through that country as safely as in N.Y.

It was a pleasing sight on the afternoon of the 8th Sept.—as I rode forward to the edge of the bluff which I saw before me, and saw a broad green valley and on the river bank the buildings and flag of Fort Shaw—the first buildings I had seen in a trail of little less than a thousand miles since leaving Fort Buford. The fort however proved on closer inspection to be not so handsome, a lot [of] squat adobe buildings all in a mass together. It is garrisoned by 6 Companies of the 7th Infantry and commanded by Gen. John Gibbon of the old 2nd Corps, now Colonel of the 7th, who although he has been in a garrison most of his life, seems to have escaped its stultifying influences, and although a Colonel, can still do something himself. He has done one thing for his post which makes it different from all others; this consists in an irrigating ditch 7 miles long. Part of it goes to the garden, the rest to the parade ground & to every officer's front yard—and everything is bright and green for half the year. The post is right in a recess, almost, of the Rocky Mtns. The buttes of the foot hills overlook the post & the main chain of the Mtns. circles around them west & south—about 40 miles off—East & Southeast are more detached mountains.

Sun river flows past the post through a fine valley already settled, and joins the Missouri in about 15 miles. Helena & its surrounding mines lie 80 miles to the South West through "the Gateway of the Mountains." The mining interests there are said to be declining but it is not in mines that Northern Montana has her wealth, it is in her grazing land. It is destined to be the great stock raising region of the country; already it rivals Texas for beef raising—both in numbers and quality and the sheep that have been introduced have done splendidly and only a little more capital is required to introduce many herds of them.

The day that I reached the post I saw probably 1000 or 1500 head of cattle running loose; there being a great many antelope in the same region I mistook them at first for buffalo. I never ate more delicious beef than that on which we have been feasting for ten days.

The ground is covered both on the hills & in the valleys with an abundant growth of the buffalo grass whose roots are green at all seasons of the year, and no attention is ever given to the cattle beyond branding in the spring & driving to market in the fall. They take care of themselves during the winter.

With a little irrigation, the soil yields splendidly and Gen.

Gibbon showed me the Post garden with a good deal of pride. Immense turnips as large as an ordinary New England squash, great clouds of cabbage heads &c. &c., all of which did not interest me very much—but the potatoes did. To one who has not seen a potato for three months, it is no slight pleasure to come across potatoes weighing 2, 3 and even 4 lbs. and seemingly possessed of some quality which makes it impossible to spoil them in cooking; I have not seen one yet —even cooked in the open air on a broken stove—that did not burst open with bright white meal.

SEPTEMBER 10TH

Having rested a day at Ft. Shaw, I started out on the 10th for Fort Benton. The first few miles of the journey—in the valley of Sun River, was through a green valley of farms & fences, a promising and flourishing country; but it was soon evident that we had only passed through a little corner of civilization, as we soon came out on the flat, browned and dusty prairie.

SEPTEMBER 11TH

I reached Fort Benton on the morning of the 11th, and found there the rest of our people, except the escort who had gone back to Buford overland.

Fort Benton is a row of whisky shanties along the river front and a few adobe buildings in the background—by all odds the lowest of all the low places I have seen on the frontier. At the other end of the "town" is a stockade of adobe garrisoned by a Company of the 7th Inf'y—the quarters propped up with sticks and so shaky and full of vermin that the men sleep outdoors and the officers seek refuge with one of the two respectable traders in town. The Great Falls of the Missouri are about 20 miles higher up and this is the first flat or bottom along the river below them—which naturally determined its location as a trading post 30 or 40 years ago, and it grew a little when steamboats began to run on the river and it figured as the head of navigation. The boats run there however only in the early season; this year 6 or 7 reached it.

There are two legitimate licensed traders in the place; but the main commerce is in whisky, this being the grand depot for the whisky which is carried over the line near the mountains & traded to the Indians there.

SEPTEMBER 12TH

I was glad to get away, which we did at noon on the day after my arrival. Our fleet of mackinaws sailed from Fort Benton at noon on the 12th. Several of the officers from Fort Shaw had come up to see us off and they and the officers of the fort gave us a salute as we passed, with an old mountain howitzer, and we answered with our carbines.

The "Mackinaw" of the north western river is not a mackinaw at all—it is simply a huge flat-bottomed New England skiff. Ours are 35 feet long, 10 feet beam and 2½ feet depth of hold—all open without any decking—made of unplaned pine boards caulked with oakum—loaded each with about 4000 lbs. We draw 10 inches of water.

In packing the boats the bow is given up to the light baggage and bedding; then come 4 seats for rowing, and under and over them are packed boxes of rations, tents &c., in the waist of the boats is the cook stove and its accompaniments, and just back of this the "bridge"—a board with cleats running across from rail to rail and on which stands the steersman. The steering oar is like that of a flat boat or raft of logs; consisting of a rail hung on an iron pin at the stern of the boat, one end of the rail is at a convenient height over the bridge and the other in the water has a board spiked to it. The space 6x6 back of the bridge is pretty well filled up with instruments, desks, boxes of records and the officer of the boat.

In each boat are an officer and assistants—or two assistants, cook and 10 men giving two reliefs at the rowing and steering oars. Twining's boat with a pilot supposed to know the river, takes the lead; my boat, which is the fourth in line, also has a pilot and the rest of the fleet of six boats follow in our wake as closely as possible, keeping a sufficient interval to have room to try a fresh place if we bring up on a bar. The regimen of this river is so eccentric that no one knows its channel, nor can know it for it exists only for the day. The whole fleet went aground yesterday in five inches of water where last year was the steamboat channel with as many feet. Independent of the larger changes each season by which the land is washed away on one side and made on the other, and the whole course of the river changed sometimes a quarter of a mile in five years, minor changes are going forward on the bars from day to day.

Our pilots however are as useful as the steamboat pilots, and like them, they steer by the eye altogether; from the color of the water and the ripples on its surface, shoal water can generally be detected and avoided; rocks and snags make themselves apparent from the break and fall of the water. Occasionally however comes a bar stretching so nearly across the river that the lead boat has to guess where the "hole" is— and very often brings up aground, the other boats with more or less success try other places.

When a boat goes aground the current generally swings the bow up stream and with the oars & tent poles we generally succeed in pushing off up stream and trying again. Sometimes the boat goes way on the bar & grounds its whole length; then there is nothing to do but all hands overboard, lift and pull either over the bar or up stream and try again. Rocks and snags are only struck by bad steering—a novice at the steering oar sees a snag ahead some distance and leisurely steers out of its way. Meantime however, the snag is as it were coming up stream as fast as he is going down, and al-

most before he knows it the current bumps him broadside
against it. Almost all the snags point down stream and as we
have not struck any backward branches, no damage has resulted from any such collisions further than the laughs of the
other crews.

Leaving Fort Benton the river took us a winding and generally northeast course for 30 miles (12 by land) to the
mouth of the Marias river, where early in the afternoon we
tied up to the bank for the night, waiting for the mail which
was to arrive in Benton during the evening. There is something rather appalling to me in the idea of a river stretching
before you continuously for such an immense distance. We
were starting on a three weeks' voyage of 1256 miles and at
the end were to be where? At Bismarck which probably
seems to you the very last place in creation. Beyond that the
river goes on and on in its endless course, scoring 3000 miles
at St. Louis and still on and on indefinitely its thousands
more to the Gulf of Mexico. The great main artery of a
continent. Near its head waters where we were it is a clear
blue stream with pebbly bottom and high sandy and clayish
banks.

September 13th

The next day we passed through the "rocky part" of the
river; bluffs 300 to 500 feet high and nearly vertical, of white
soft sandstone worn by time and weather into strange shapes,
and many slender pinnacles balancing large boulders on
their points; and running through this in all sorts of curious
directions were large veins of dark trap, running down into
the river like steep stone fences. Occasionally we came to a
bluff all of trap, not unlike in shape and color, the Palisades
of the Hudson; and our boats dwarfed in size at the base and
with the stove pipes puffing in the centre, reminded me
strongly of the pictures of Fulton's first steamboat.

It was a bright cloudless afternoon, the temperature just

comfortable and the splendid bracing atmosphere of the North West. As we floated down past the bluffs, without a ripple on the water, no sound but the regular r-r-r-r-ruck r-r-r-r-ruck of the oars, the setting sun lighting up the white sandstone cliffs in front of us in contrast to the dark trap, and an occasional fringe of green cottonwood near the water for color—not a sign of life but the mountain sheep staring at us from the peaks—it all formed a weird and witching scene—the only part of our voyage to be remembered with much pleasure, for the never failing Equinoctial storm is only a few days from us and has already given us a few premonitory drenchings.

That day—the 13th—we turned the big northern bend and winding to the Southeast tied up for the night at dark, opposite Hole in the Wall, having travelled 85 miles of river and about 50 by land.

47° 49′ 02″ 7
110° 01′ 17″ 8.

A bright starlit night, no tents were pitched, but after the observations were taken we gathered around a huge fire, then rolled out our blankets and slept soundly till day break. We revel in the abundance of water and fuel—two necessaries which have been so scanty this summer—to say nothing of magnificent beef and potatoes, of which we had nearly forgotten the taste.

Two of my assistants in the rearmost boat are constantly engaged all day in making a reconnaissance survey of the river with compass and chronometer, estimating the distances from time. Every clear night I observe for latitude and longitude; all the chronometers of the survey have been turned over to me and I expect to get very good longitudes from them, & there is no trouble in observing the latitude within 500 ft.; so that if we have clear nights I expect to get a very good reconnaissance map of the river—better at all events than has ever been obtained.

The only surveys ever made are two; the exploration of Lewis & Clark in 1804 which was very inaccurate, and Capt. Raynolds' survey—Capt. Raynolds (now Lt. Col. of our corps) in 1859 made a reconnaissance of the Yellowstone, thence across towards the mountains and down the river from Benton to Buford in a single boat in Sept. 1859. He got I think only 5 latitude observations and as he travelled about as rapidly as we do, his survey was, I suppose, made in a similar manner. His map is the only map of the upper Missouri.

We often think of the Lewis & Clark expedition and it seems to me a more adventuresome journey than that of Columbus & almost as valuable. Seventy years ago, in 1804 these two men with a small party, left St. Louis, then a mere trading post in the far, far West "beyond the Alleghenies," to explore the great North West, an entirely unknown country. They started out with provisions for 18 months, in open boats similar to ours; occasionally they were able to sail but most of the way were obliged to "cordel"—i.e. haul their boats by ropes from the shore.

The first winter they reached old Ft. Mandan, a trading post near the present site of Bismarck and stayed there till spring. Next year they came on, passed successfully through all the hostile Indian tribes on the river, found its head waters in the Three Forks which they named after Jefferson, Madison and Gallatin, pushed on across the summit of the mountains to the main forks of the Columbia which they named respectively the Lewis & Clark forks; & wintered there; next year they followed the Columbia down and reached the Pacific. For two years and a half they had been travelling through absolutely unknown & unheard of country inhabited only by savages; and driving off starvation and sickness mostly as savages do. It was an expedition which for pluck and skill has no equal in our history and never can have again, for there is now no such extent of country unexplored on the face of the globe except possibly in the heart of Africa.

SEPTEMBER 14TH

At 4 o'clock in the morning of the 14th the camp guards began calling out among the heaps of blankets, "Roll out, tumble out, daylight!!"—and each in turn poked his nose out from under his buffalo robe, and rubbing his eyes; probably every man without exception wanted very strongly to poke his nose back again. But out we tumbled, yawned, shivered, & rapidly got inside of our skin breeches and overcoats, rolled up the blankets and in half an hour, in the gray twilight of a clear frosty morning we were off again. Breakfast was ready in half an hour more and eaten with the most manifest relish. Landing for half an hour's rest about 7 o'clock and then again we were finally under way for the day.

The trap rock of the preceding day soon disappeared and before noon we missed the sandstone also; the bluffs now reduced to simon-pure "bad lands" of dull clay, the bottom of the river seldom pebbly, generally mud, and the bars of this spring three feet out of water of soft silt. A strong head wind early in the morning rendered steering very difficult, as the oars could only just keep the boat even with the current. The bluffs were covered with the mountain pine and on their steep sides all the morning we passed flock after flock of mountain sheep who stared at us and seemed but little disturbed by our presence. Having plenty of meat on hand and no surplus ammunition, Twining had given positive orders against any shooting, and we reluctantly passed many of them at less than 300 yards.

About noon quite a bright and animated scene was before us, the first signs of human life on the voyage. We were approaching quite a large camp of Crows & Gros Ventres, and a log trading post in the centre. On each side of us the valley was quite wide, the Judith River—a considerable stream from the south—emptying here. Some years ago there was a garrison here, the post being called Camp Cooke. As we approached there were 8 or 10 lodges on either side of the river and just below them a large number of squaws, papooses, men & ponies crossing the river—their household effects packed on the lodge poles, making what is called a "travois" and drawn by the ponies who swam the river, often with a squaw astride and two papooses on her back. The squaws, & half naked little urchins stared at us from the bank and an immense pack of dogs gave us sweet music as we rowed past, but the men paid but little attention.

One splendidly muscular young buck, sitting bareback on a fine pony, clothed simply in a shirt, who seemed to be directing the crossing, formed a fine subject for a sketch. The old Chief, gorgeous in scarlet & white and mounted on a spotted brown horse of the kind so much esteemed by circus spectators and Indians, rode along on the bank opposite us for some distance, followed by his sons and one or two head men similarly mounted. Apparently they were expecting us to stop and have a talk but we declined their hospitality and kept on. These two bands number about 300 men and perhaps 1500 or more souls in all. They have long been at peace with the whites and are considered "a very decent band of Indians." They were well clad and the herd of about 600 ponies contained the best looking Indian ponies I have seen.

Their country ranges along the river east to the Musselshell where they run against the Sioux & northwest to the Sweet Grass Hills where they strike the Blackfeet. Near this point we found 22 corpses on the boundary line, they belonged to this band & were killed by the Piegans this last spring. Their bodies were riddled by bullets, scalped and horribly mutilated of course.

After leaving the Gros Ventres Camp the banks of the river gradually began to assume the character which they have below—dull monotonous clay bad lands. Numerous flocks of sheep were seen on them however, and later in the afternoon several herds of buffalo crossing the river. We almost succeeded in running down two old bulls who were swimming strongly before us. At every brushy point we passed we heard the shrill whistle of the elk, with which the river abounds. We only saw two bands of them but heard them all day & every day since in fact. Black tailed & red deer were also seen feeding along the bank—one of them was shot by Twining's pilot.

It is a magnificent game country all along this part of the river, and we regretted very much not having a day or two to devote to them, the elk particularly. The pilots show us the points on the river as we go along with the remark "Two men killed there in '70. Three men killed there in '69 &c &c." The most interesting was the mouth of the Musselshell where at a woodyard (for steamboats) three men were killed this month by Sioux. All these men were almost entirely alone, one or two of them locating a hut on some point & chopping wood for the steamboats. It is risky work but the wood brings a high price.

North bank just west of creek above Sturgeon Island.

47° 46′ 53″ 5
109° 09′ 22″ 3.

SEPTEMBER 16TH

On the morning of the 16th near Carroll as we emerged from our robes the sky was very black & cloudy, and half an hour after we were under way it began to rain hard & soon wet us through. After that the best thing to do was to keep on rowing, which we did all day. You can imagine the misery of being in an open boat, crowded with men, baggage, rations & a little of everything, and staying there for 10 hours quietly absorbing a pelting rain. We officers in the stern sheets managed to get a little shelter from tents & spare can-

vas but the men stuck to their oars all day; & eagerly counted
the minutes to the time for their relief to pull and get
warmed up. It held up somewhat just before dark and as we
went into camp opposite the mouth of the Musselshell, the
stars were shining brightly; and we partially forgot our
troubles before a blazing cottonwood fire.

$$47° \ 27' \ 56'' \ 1$$
$$107° \ 54' \ 32'' \ 8.$$

SEPTEMBER 17TH

All signs however fail in this latitude at this season, and in
spite of a very handsome semi-circular rainbow just at sun-
down, we woke up the next morning (17th) to see the sky
jet black, and a rainbow in the west—and our moist misery
recommenced & lasted till noon, then a little clear sky until
about 4 o'clock a very black cloud in the North made us seek
the first landing and get our tents up before the gale & rain
struck us. It did not rain very hard but it blew a hurricane
from the North all night.

SEPTEMBER 18TH

In the morning it was still blowing violently but in our
favor and we hastened to take advantage of it. It is a little
ambiguous to say of the wind that it was in our favor on a
river whose course points to every one of the 360 degrees of
direction in half a day's travel, but by good fortune, we were
at the head of the only straight piece of river on the map.
Between the 107th and 108th meridian the river keeps a
nearly due easterly course for 20 miles with no appreciable
bends, ending at Round Butte, a pointed hill on the south
bank, making a well-known landmark. The wind was due
west and we improvised a good many yards of sail from tents
& flies. We scudded along about 7 miles an hour with sails &
oars, and at noon passed the Round Butte—which is halfway

between Benton & Buford. The weather finally cleared up during the afternoon and has since been delightful.

North bank halfway between Round Butte & Fort Peck.

$$47° 47' 01'' 7$$
$$106° 38' 56'' 8.$$

SEPTEMBER 19TH

About noon on the 19th we arrived at Fort Peck. It is an event to meet any living things on our voyage down this great lone river, but Fort Peck is particularly remarkable as one of the largest Indian Agencies in the whole country—rations being issued now to 800 families, about 6000 souls. As we approached, their new white lodges stood out against the sky on top of the dusty brown hills and a few ponies were seen picking up what little grass they could. Wrapped up in blankets and suspended on poles outside of camp we could see several "good Indians" (dead).

On turning the next bend the stockade came in sight on a little flat at the bottom of the bluffs. The stockade was large —enclosing nearly an acre—as it must be to hold the stores for 6000 people. In front of it were two or three hundred men & boys more or less gaudily dressed in scarlet blankets, worked with colored porcupine quills; they loafed about staring at the white men's boats; while off on one side the squaws and dogs were hauling water up to camp.

I naturally attracted quite a crowd by taking out my sextant to get a latitude; they crowded around at a respectful distance in large number to see "the white man make big medicine." After I had finished one old fellow came up to me with a grave face, holding a chip on which was a small drop of mercury which had been dropped in putting it up. How long he had spent in picking it off the ground I don't know.

Inside the stockade was a trader's store full of hides and robes; and blankets & saddles to exchange for more of them.

The trader's house had some of the handsomest quill work in it I have ever seen; I was sorry not to be able to get some of it but it was not for sale.

They spoke of the ammunition trade being very strictly prohibited, but I noticed a fine Henry rifle and a belt full of cartridges on about half the men. This large number of Indians are all Sioux. Nine bands in all, Yanktons, Unca-papas, Tetons, Cutheads, Assiniboines & several others.

Many of them were on the boundary last summer, stole from the English depots, chased one of our mail riders all day & did several other exploits. They are a bad lot. Only a month ago they put four bullets in one of the Agency employees a mile from the stockade. I saw the man & heard his story—an entirely unprovoked outrage. He knows the men but is powerless to have them punished.

As I looked at these great strapping young bucks idling along the river, it struck me very forcibly what a strange idea to feed & clothe a thousand able-bodied men and their large families simply to make them do nothing. Year in and year out they have absolutely nothing to do—and they *do nothing,* except a small party of young bucks steals off now & then in the night to kill any stray white man they may meet, steal his horses & do any deviltry which will give them reputation. No punishments are inflicted on them as far as I can learn, for mischief.

They are not given any thing to do and seem to be simply required to do nothing. The river above them abounds in game of all kinds but they never hunt—why should they? It requires work and patience to kill an elk but it is very little trouble to walk over to the Agency, draw a sack of flour and a quarter of beef and load them up on a squaw to carry to the lodge.

After leaving Fort Peck and the Indians we wound around for a couple of hours only to find that the river had brought us back to them again and half a mile from where we left them before. Waving them once more an affectionate adieu, we floated along round and round and round again through the bends till we were almost dizzy.

A little before dark we passed the mouth of the Milk River of which we have seen so much this summer. It empties in a considerable delta and has formed so large a bar at its mouth as to force the river across a bend opposite to it. The river first cut its way through this bend three years ago and now it is the main channel.

Here the bluffs on the river bank quite disappeared and a more uninteresting country than that we passed over in the next two days can hardly be found. The river spread out in places to a mile and a half and two miles in width, a channel near each shore and the rest a few inches of water or open bar. Standing up in the boat we could just see over the banks across a dead flat as far as the eye could reach; the water and the banks all of the same color—the color of mud; not a ripple on the surface and the sun beating down with July force.

North bank about 3 miles below mouth of Milk River.

$$48° 01' 36'' 8$$
$$106° 13' 47'' 8.$$

September 20th

The next afternoon we passed another curious phase of this eccentric river—viz. the "Fort Charles cutoff." At one point we saw the cut banks and broad shallow bed of the former stream bearing off to the south and half a mile further on the same thing returning north again. My pilot had been past this place three years ago and then went through the old channel and the cut-off did not exist. Now the old channel is quite dry and all the water goes through the cut-off. As the old bend was 12 miles around & the cut-off ½ mile, we sighed for more cut-offs.

It seems a great waste of force that such an immense body of water as this should flow through such a wretched alluvial bottom as to render it navigable only for such miserable light draft stern wheel steamboats as ply on it. If this amount of water were confined within hard banks a quarter of a mile apart it would float the fleets of the world nearly to Fort Benton. As it is, the banks are powerless before the force of the water.

The water comes down some spring and leaving its former channel abuts against some bank covered with immense cottonwood trees, and cuts it off like a paring machine; sometimes 100 yards in one season; the trees drop to the bottom, their roots become fastened in the mud & their trunks form formidable snags, so thick as to give the appearance of the teeth in a harrow; as the current goes here a bar forms opposite, where the water eddies, and the only channel is right through these snags, from one to another of which the boat must bump with slackened speed in order to get through at all.

The two or three acres of ground thus torn off the river carries on for a few miles to the next bend where on the convex side the eddying current deposits it as a bar and in the fall it stands three feet out of water—silt without consistency enough to support a dog. Leaving it a year or two to harden a little in the autumn suns, the river comes along some spring higher and stronger than usual and cuts its main channel 20 feet deep and 100 yards wide, right through the centre of it— and so on from year to year in endless change, cutting away here and building there, only to remodel it the next year— as if never satisfied with itself. In the long ages that the river has been flowing I suppose that every foot of its broad valley has at some time been the bed of the stream.

How man can change the course of nature in all this is a tremendous problem, and as the country begins to be settled

—and there is no doubt of the fine country about the head waters of this river being settled in a few years—it becomes a problem requiring immediate solution. I don't see what the solution is going to be—dredging, wing dams and dikes being quite out of the question from expense alone on a length of 2000 miles with a bar every half mile & constantly shifting. As I said before it seems a terrible waste that a river stretching from the ocean right through a continent to its very centre and containing water enough to float the largest ships in the world if only confined, should from the mere waywardness of its course be accessible only to tuppenny steam flat boats.

About five miles below Ft. Charles Cut-Off.

$$48° 04' 11'' 8$$
$$105° 32' 32'' 8.$$

SEPTEMBER 21ST

On the 21st of September we passed the mouth of Poplar River up which you may remember I made a trail to the boundary last summer; and that night camped at French-man's Point where I had left the other parties.

About 5 miles above Frenchman's Point:

$$48° 06' 02''$$
$$104° 55' 46'' 3.$$

SEPTEMBER 22ND

The next day at noon we passed the Big Muddy & I stopped long enough to walk over and look at my bridge of last summer. The (Big Muddy) river now had only a few inches of water in it but the soft mud was several feet deep. The bridge *was there* and the 200 wagons which have now crossed it have sunk the sills so deep into the mud that like snags in the river, I don't think the spring freshets can dislodge them at all.

North bank about 3 miles above mouth of Little Muddy River.

$$48° \ 03' \ 12'' \ 5$$
$$104° \ 10' \ 59'' \ 8.$$

SEPTEMBER 23RD

The second morning afterwards we passed the mouth of the Yellowstone. Recent rains had made the Missouri—which is usually clear at this season—quite muddy and there was no difference in the colors of the two streams as they mingled; their width was about equal. I wrote last summer that the Yellowstone was the main stream and was the head of the Mississippi.

I was a little mistaken about this and the Missouri is probably the main stream; to the mouth of the Yellowstone the length of both is about the same, but the Yellowstone *never has been* navigated more than 200 miles above its mouth while the Missouri is navigable for 800 miles above this point.

Turning the bend at the mouth of the Yellowstone, Fort Buford loomed up in front like a large city and precisely at noon of the 23rd we landed; 11 days exactly from Ft. Benton, 800 miles by water and 400 by land.

The infantry of our escort had arrived overland three days before and they and Gen. Hazen received us most cordially, their white shirts and clean clothes forming a strong contrast to our semi-barbaric mud-colored buck skins and woolen shirts. Our only consolation was in remembering that a month ago they were as much mudstained as ourselves and that our day of white shirts & shaved faces is only a week or so ahead.

Gen Hazen is Colonel of the 6th Inf'y—also author of "The School & the Army in Germany and France in 1870," in which you remember the Engineers & Ordnance and all the staff corps are very summarily dealt with. But I had no hard feelings against him as he spoke dolefully of his lot, planted out here in the remote frontier and quite as effectually planted and with as little to do as if he were five feet under ground. He and all the officers were as cordial and hospitable as possible and pressed us warmly to stay over night, but we knew too well the allurements of a post; we got a fresh supply of rations; & just before dark, to the music of a fine band, we hauled down the river a mile or more, so as to get an early start in the morning.

$$47° \; 59' \; 09'' \; 8$$
$$103° \; 57' \; 04'' \; 5 \; (?).$$

SEPTEMBER 24TH

The 24th of September was bright and cloudless, and the sun poured down on the water with such dazzling light and heat that I was forced to set Mother Invention to work to rig an awning over the stern of the boat, and a great comfort it was; giving me also a nice place to sleep under on the boat which of course did away with the necessity of getting up till breakfast time.

We were wondering what had become of our equinoctial storm which is never known to fail in this country; and here it was the 24th of September bright and clear and hot as June and nothing yet but two days rain a week ago.

South bank.

$$48° \; 01' \; 41'' \; 3$$
$$103° \; 27' \; 02'' \; 8.$$

SEPTEMBER 25TH

But we had only to wait till the next day, when about 9 in the morning, running southeast, a furious gale struck us from the northwest. I pulled in the oars and hoisted sail, but hardly had I got it up when I saw that we could not carry it and while trying to take it down, bang went the mast, shot in two at the middle amid the yells of the other crews. Half shipwrecked in a gale of wind and our eyes full of *dust!!*—it certainly was an amphibious arrangement of circumstances; the gale had all the force of a gale at sea for coming from a little west of north there was nothing to break its force between the polar sea and ourselves; and coming over the sand bars in the middle of the stream it picked up such a cloud of dust that we could hardly see the other boats. Scudding a few miles before the wind brought us around the bend and in the teeth of the wind, and now with two men at each oar and the current with us it was nip and tuck for an hour whether we would get over the mile of water ahead—and a fair probability that tuck would get the best of it.

We did finally get to the head of the bend about noon and let the men rest and get their dinner, and we rigged a guy mast in my boat for half a sail—all we could carry.

Starting ahead again before the wind on another bend, we had the satisfaction in the first five minutes of yelling at three successive boats as their masts snapped in two and their colors and sail dropped in the water as we went scudding past.

This left me ahead with no boat in front whose mistakes I could take advantage of (my pilot, by the way, had left at Buford) and it was ticklish work. We were going along about 8 miles an hour through the water and the current 3 miles more, and we must look out for bars a long way ahead or we would be on them before we knew it. If we struck a soft bar we would go on it so far that nothing but all hands overboard and a long haul back would get us off; if we struck anything hard we would go to pieces. On we went charging along however with no misfortune, myself and the strongest man in the boat having all we could do at the tiller, fine sport it was and made me think with delight of my boyhood days a dozen years ago on Narragansett Bay.

After an hour or so of this I saw ahead a steamboat blown

on to the mud on the lee shore. Taking down the sail and backing water I went on board & found it to be the "Fontenelle" on which we had gone up the river last summer. We had no desire to change with them, from this point to Buford we had been 2½ days *against* the current last summer; coming *down* in our boats with wind & current we had been only 1½ days. We also learned that she had been 7 *weeks* last summer making the round trip from Bismarck to Benton and back. On board we found several officers & their wives and the wives of others going to rejoin their husbands who had been out with us this summer.

The sky had been jet black all day—as much as we could see of it through the clouds of dust, and we were momentarily expecting the snow or rain, but to our surprise, as we tied up for the night at dark, the wind calmed down and the sky cleared off.

North bank about 4 miles above mouth of White Earth River.

48° 06′ 56″ 7 (?)

102° 44′ 56″ 8.

SEPTEMBER 26TH

During the night however, the gale came on again and just after starting we spent another wearying two hours pulling up to the head of a bend, & began to think that the wind did us more harm than good. Resting here before starting down the bend, I rigged a mast 6 inches through and geared it to the boat so that it could not go without tearing the boat to pieces; with the old mast we put a small leg of mutton sail in the bow to help the steering and a lee board over the side to keep from drifting, and now starting a mile behind the fleet we soon went flying past each boat in succession.

Noon found us tugging hard again at the oars "up a bend" and a well earned rest after it. The wind was now blowing harder than ever—a perfect tempest; and when we started again with half a tent fly (10'x10')—all the sail we could carry, as we went flying along, the men alternately held their breath and laughed to see the water go by. In about an hour we were going dead before the wind full 10 miles an hour beside the current, and the dust so thick that we could not see where we were going.

Presently I discerned ahead a boat aground on a bar and in as many seconds the man sounding in the bow of my boat called out "Two feet, foot and a half, one foot, nine inches" and with a lurch and a swash of the water we came to a stand still. Thinking I could go over with such a wind, I called to the men to pull hard at the oars, and a gust of wind striking us just then the boat seemed to lift itself and drop again a boat's length ahead—but in four inches of water and we draw ten!! High & dry we were now and the wind whistling past; the other boats went past us like feathers in a gale—and for us there was nothing to do but all hands overboard in the mud, lift the boat up, and literally carry it—a few inches at a time—back into deep water; it was a half hour's operation; and then we went scudding on again. It was certainly an odd sight on the "Wild Missouri," this furious gale, not a cloud in the sky but immense clouds of dust in our eyes, the waves large enough on the long bends to wash occasionally into the boat, and the bank flying past us as if bewitched. And stranger than all, the wind went down at sunset, not a cloud in the sky.

North east bank at mouth of a creek below Shell Creek.

$$47° \ 46' \ 07'' \ 5$$
$$102° \ 15' \ 46'' \ 3.$$

SEPTEMBER 27TH

Today, September 27th, is a bright calm, cloudless day, the sun pouring down on the water and the perspiration streaming off the oarsmen. Our equinoctial storm this year has got lost.

We are nearing the Mandan Indian village at Fort Berthold and expect to be at Bismarck in 2 days more.

North bank around the sharp bend below Berthold and about 3 miles east of the Fort in a straight line.

$$47° 31' 27'' 5$$
$$101° 45' 47'' 8 (?).$$

SEPTEMBER 29TH

A few hours after I stopped writing day before yesterday, we came to another large Agency, Fort Berthold, where is a village of 2200 Mandans and Rees, friends of the whites and deadly enemies of the Sioux. The Mandans are making some little progress in civilization—as much I think as any Indians known except the Cherokees. They have fenced off a farm a mile square and grow "forty day" corn, potatoes & a few other vegetables. The squaws of course do most of the work.

They live in very decent hovels known as "Mandan houses." Large posts are set in the ground in a circle thirty feet in diameter and these are connected with inclined poles & brush;—the whole is then covered with mud, leaving a hole in the top for the smoke to escape, after the manner of an ordinary skin lodge.

The mud bakes in the sun and makes them light & warm and very good houses—for Indians. Inside, the ground is bare and a fire in the centre, but I was surprised to find a dozen or more wooden bedsteads against the sides—more properly "bunks" like those in a barrack—and all *curtained* with skins or cloth; and above all, on some beds, were sheets quite decently white!!

The Mandans too are quite noted as the only Northern Indians who make any pottery. It is not elaborate, simple earthen pots with ears, made from the Missouri clay &

moulded by hand. The Agent gave me one as a specimen. Another curious feature in this village is a young Ree who has learned his trade as a carpenter and blacksmith; and is said to be an excellent one. I saw some carts made by him which certainly were very creditable, particularly the iron work.

Altogether, this is quite a hopeful lot of Indians, but still so terribly far behind civilization.

While we were there, there was a big dance going on among the young bucks, and we went over to see it. The house was crowded with a circle of men against the sides as thick as they could squeeze—probably 30 in all squatting on their haunches; young men between 20 and 30 years old. Their attire was the most fantastic I have ever seen—not that there was much clothing about it, most of them having on only breech clout, moccasins & war bonnets—but the variety of apparel that was painted on their bodies defies all cataloguing.

Beginning at the head, the war bonnet is made of eagle feathers, each feather denoting a scalp taken by the wearer. There were only a few of these, the other bonnets being old soldiers' hats &c. The paint began on the forehead & covered the body to the feet. One man presented quite a bizarre appearance by having a first coat of blue from head to foot; on this were stripes in various directions of red. One eye was set in a circle of brick red and the other in sky blue; broad bands of red connected his mouth and ears, from which hung earrings two inches in diameter. His arms were striped somewhat after the manner of a clown in the circus; his back was divided into red and blue by his spine; and his legs were a work of art; being most elaborately divided into diamonds and looking like tesselated pavement. The rest of the band were carefully decorated but hardly equal to this chef d'oeuvre. Some had moustaches & beards painted on their faces, others had the eyebrows arched, and others again were most delicately rouged! Jewelry in the shape of earrings, finger rings, bracelets and *anklelets,* size apparently being the chief consideration in their selection.

On one side were the professional musicians, six in number, with grave faces intent on their work, which consisted in beating an immense tom tom and chanting a monotonous sort of low yell. When the music waxed loud the bucks all jumped out in the middle and danced; the step being a scrape and a hop without turning, the knees being always bent, and all singing. When they got out of breath they all gave a loud hi! with a tremendous bang on the drum and then sat down & kept passing around a single pipe.

And now for a commentary on their civilization. While the gaudily attired young men were enjoying themselves, in came an old ragged *squaw* carrying a large iron pot of coffee and a large pile on her back which when unrolled proved to be a huge tray of hoe cakes—this was the feast. As soon as the woman had deposited her burdens she went out and the dance went on. The only woman's rights the noble red man recognizes are the right to do all the housework, chop wood, bring water; do the garden work, take care of the children—what little care the naked urchins get—and make her master's beadwork.

I have seen a good many of these dances, among the Chippewas, the Gros Ventres & the Mandans and they all seem to me alike and equally meaningless. I have often asked what the point of them was, what they signified; but have never received any tangible answer. They told me this was the "Grass Dance" a peaceable amusement of the young bucks. It seemed to me utterly senseless, but when we remember how much enjoyment some men derive from participating in a muddy Broadway procession, or what delight an Irishman takes in a funeral—why it is not so very strange after all.

I suppose that this dance was the dim representative in the savage mind of a young man's dinner party "evening dress!"

[Observations taken September 29th, East Bank.]

47° 07′ 08″ 7
100° 55′ 50″ 8.

September 30th

We are nearing Bismarck and "now my tale is ended." As we sat around our last camp fire last night, my mind ran back over these last two years, eighteen months of which I have spent "on the prairie," and I can only say I heartily wish I had more of it to look forward to. I don't know that I ever enjoyed myself more.

Rough and wild you may call the life—and so it is externally, but it need not have any hardening effect on one's mind. The hardships of it become mere pastime to a young man of health and energy—an outlet for his superfluous activity. And the freedom of it is dear indeed; to escape from the trammels of society to feel perfectly independent of the thousand and one little requirements which are not points of fine breeding but mere superficial conventionalities, to get out of the narrow rut into which most young people drift in city life, to feel occasionally that your safety depends on your judgment and endurance; and finally the independence and self-reliance which come from being thrown so much on your own resources; the exhilaration of breathing such pure health-giving air—all this, as accessory to scientific work which goes on record with your name and which at any time you can refer to with pride, forms an experience which has exceeded the most sanguine anticipations which I formed when I received my detail two years and a half ago in the swamps of North Carolina.

Tied up 2 P.M. at freight wharf termination of switch about 2½ miles N.W. of Bismarck. 100° 49′ 36″ 6. The latitude & longitude of Bismarck were determined with

Zenith Telescope & Transit & telegraph from Chicago by Col. Barlow in 1872 or '73, and were published in Annual Report, Ch'f Eng'r for 1874.

Arrived here—1256 miles of river in 18 days and 2 hours.

Aff'ly,
F. V. G.

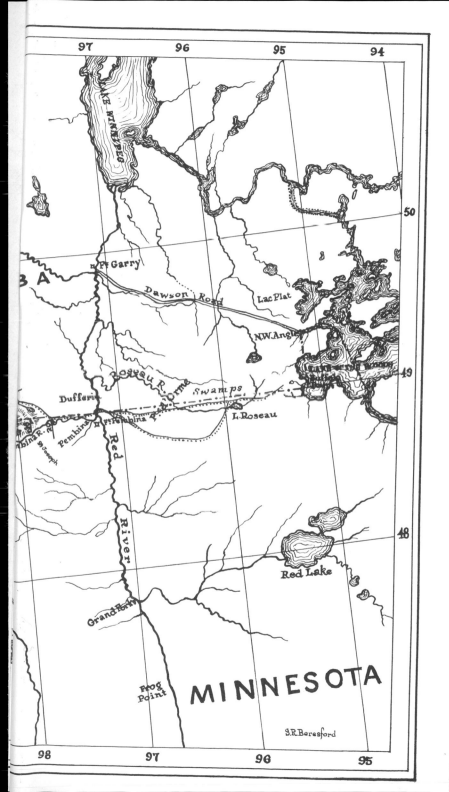

INDEX

DATE DUE

F
597
N83

22275

F.
597   22275
N83   Parsons

West on the 49 th
parallel.

DATE	ISSUED TO

F
597 Parsons
N83   West on the 49th parallel.

22275

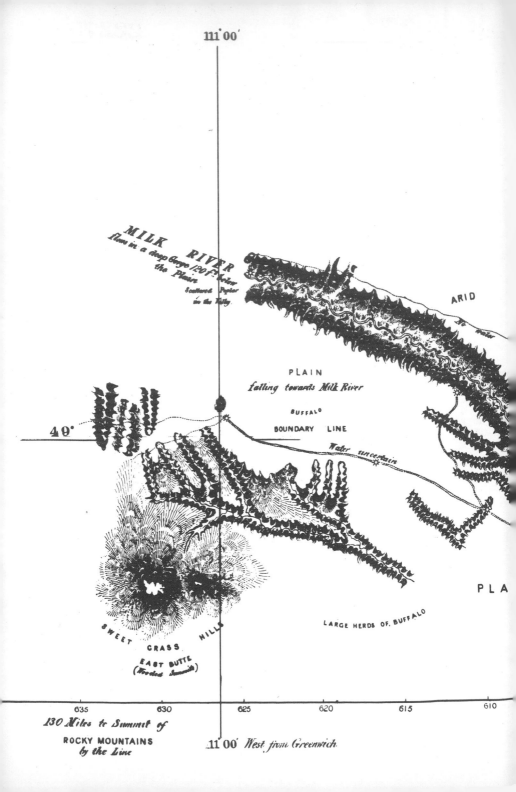

111° 00'

MILK RIVER
flows in a deep Gorge 120 ft. below
the Plain

Scattered Poplar
in the Valley.

ARID

PLAIN
falling towards Milk River

BUFFALO

BOUNDARY LINE

Water uncertain

40°

PLA

LARGE HERDS OF. BUFFALO

SWEET GRASS HILLS

EAST BUTTE
(*Wooded Summit*)

635 630 625 620 615 610

130 Miles to Summit of
ROCKY MOUNTAINS
by the Line

11° 00' West from Greenwich.